Global Issues and Change

Global Issues and Change

Boyd Johnson and John S. Johnson

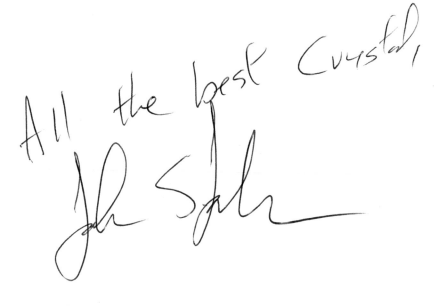

Triangle Publishing
Marion, Indiana

Global Issues and Change
Boyd Johnson and John S. Johnson

Direct correspondence, inquiries and permission requests as follows:

Triangle Publishing
Indiana Wesleyan University
4301 South Washington Street
Marion, Indiana 46953

Web site: www.trianglepublishing.com
E-mail: info@trianglepublishing.com

Johnson, Boyd and Johnson, John S.
Global Issues and Change

ISBN: 1-931283-07-9

Photographs in *Global Issues and Change* are provided with permission from Wesleyan Publishing House, Wesleyan World Missions, and the authors' personal collections.

Cover and graphic design: Lyn Rayn

Printed in the United States of America
Evangel Press, Nappanee, Indiana

Table of Contents

Introduction

Buddhist temples are a common sight in Thailand.

"How Could This Be?"

While living and working in Bangkok, Thailand, co-author Boyd Johnson visited a major slum in the city. Without food, jobs, or education, the residents lived in shacks over an open sewer. The purpose of Boyd's visit was to help initiate a project that would enable these people to improve their lives.

Later that day, Boyd attended a dinner at the Oriental Hotel, which travelers consistently rated the world's best hotel. The meal was an incredible feast of many courses, prepared by some of the world's finest chefs. After the dinner, he and the other guests were invited to the Presidential Suite, where the businessman/host was staying. True to its name, this magnificent set of rooms that took up half the hotel's top floor had recently been occupied by the President of the United States.

As Boyd stood on the balcony of the suite high over Bangkok, he looked toward the slum area he had visited that morning. The contrast between the two scenes was almost too much for him to comprehend. The one environment embodied desperate poverty, while the other represented more wealth than most people could ever imagine. Yet, they both existed in the same city—almost within walking distance of one another. How could this be? Why did such differences exist, with such great need on the one hand and such great wealth on the other?

These two extremes represent, in a microcosm, the contrasts of our world today. As we hope to demonstrate in this book, the needs are very great and affect everyone in some way. While it is important to understand the origins and ramifications of this global reality, it is not enough simply to be aware of the world's context. This knowledge also should inspire action. To develop an effective response, people must be aware of the characteristics of change. With this knowledge, they can focus action and achieve real results. It is for this reason that we have written *Global Issues and Change*.

As teachers at the university level, we also wanted to give our students a general introduction to the broad subject of global issues, with an emphasis on practical ways to both inspire and facilitate change in the world. We had been unable to find a textbook that put these concepts together in a clear and concise way, prompting our determination to write a new book that would meet this need.

Why study global issues? The answer should be evident in newspaper headlines and television news broadcasts. In some way we all are affected by international events and should know more about the world in which we live. Ignorance of what is happening beyond our national borders is no longer an option—we are interconnected in a global economy, a global environment, and a global culture. But there are other reasons besides self-interest to pursue a greater knowledge in this area. By learning more about international issues, we can make informed choices, help others, and make a difference in our world.

> By learning more about international issues, we can make informed choices, help others, and make a difference in our world.

Global Issues and Change is meant to inform and challenge the reader. The key word in each chapter title is *understanding*—an essential first step in making any kind of change, and one intended to lead the reader to see the world in a new way. Although the world is a very complicated place, we hope to add clarity without oversimplifying the complexities of either the range of global issues or the methods of change.

About the Authors

A writer's experience naturally influences how she or he sees the world. In the case of *Global Issues and Change*, we acknowledge that our perspectives have been shaped by a Western, American worldview and are influenced by our gender (male), race (white), education (graduate level), profession (teaching), and religious faith (Christian). However, this worldview has been modified in both cases by our extensive international experience in cross-cultural work and research, including international travel, living in other cultures, cross-cultural training, learning other languages, and having friends from many countries. Over the course of thirty-five combined years, the experience of encountering different ways of living and viewing the world has had a powerful effect on both of us, leading to an ongoing interest in culture and how it shapes our perception of what is right and even true. All of these experiences have provided opportunities to see things from different perspectives and to become more open to other points of view. That wider perspective is what we hope to present in this book.

John S. Johnson, Ph.D., is a member of the business faculty at Indiana Wesleyan University, where he currently teaches International Management and Organizational Behavior. He is also a human resource analyst for Global Talent International, an Indiana-based training and recruiting company. His doctorate is in intercultural education, with a focus on organizational leadership. He also holds a master's degree in human resource leadership. Previously, he worked for the

International Institute for Cooperative Studies, training business people in the Ukraine for five years. As a professor at Azusa Pacific University, he conducted leadership seminars for business people and nonprofit leaders around the world. During the seven years that he resided outside the United States, he lived in Guatemala, Nigeria, England, and Ukraine, and visited over forty countries.

Boyd Johnson, Ph.D., is an associate professor of international studies at Indiana Wesleyan University, where he teaches global issues and social science courses. His doctorate is in international studies. He previously worked for World Vision, first as a researcher at the International Office and later as Associate Director of Leadership (South Pacific), Operations (Thailand), and Training (South Asia Region). He then became the Field Director in Pakistan and later served as Director of Strategic Resources for World Vision Canada. He worked in international development for sixteen years, a position that took him to over fifty countries on all continents. He lived for thirteen years in Australia, Thailand, Pakistan, Singapore, and Canada. He also designed many community development programs and has served as a consultant to global businesses and aid agencies.

The combination of our backgrounds and training should underscore the credibility of *Global Issues and Change*. Because we both have direct knowledge and experience of the conditions we describe in each chapter, we have a great interest in encouraging and facilitating change around the world. We strongly believe that all people can make a positive impact, and should become more informed about where their skills can be used. In a way, this book has been forming itself in our minds for many years. The need for something like this became more and more evident to us as we traveled and taught in this field. We both wish that a book on these subjects had been available when we began our studies and work!

Global Issues and Change reflects our attitude on other topics as well. For example, we believe that global poverty is not just a problem for others "out there," but an issue that ultimately affects everyone, regardless of nationality. What impacts one part of the globe can easily spill over to other areas. If people are poor and have no resources, their participation in the world economy is limited. If they are hungry and have no medicine, they are more prone to disease. If people are desperate and feel they have no future, they can become open to violent solutions. All of these potential results may impact people in other nations (including the United States), even if they think it is someone else's problem. We also believe that while change is critical, it must be incorporated appropriately so that it does not harm cultures or destroy important traditions.

This Book's Approach

Global Issues and Change addresses several issues. First, we offer a brief overview of current global issues to enhance a better understanding of the world today. This includes selected topics that are of particular importance, such as information on the subject of globalization. Second, we examine American culture to offer a better understanding of this unique people, their heritage, their values, and their beliefs. Our purpose is to demonstrate how this society has created and sustains a particular worldview—a certain way of seeing the world. Third, we cover a selected number of major global needs in order to explain why everyone should be involved in change.

This then leads to an in-depth consideration of change itself. We examine various theories of change, along with practical steps for putting them into practice. This includes profiles of people who have made a difference in the world. Thus, *Global Issues and Change* does not just recite facts, but demonstrates how these facts can be used. Throughout the book we ask two questions: "What are the main global issues that we need to be aware of?" and "What change is possible?" Keep

Globalization makes it essential to understand other people.

these questions in mind, as the answers not only relate to the issues in one's life, but also provide keys for making this a better world.

If we were to summarize the main themes of the book, we would label them "the world" and "facilitating change." These two ideas are in some ways separate, and can be studied that way. We choose to place them together because we see them as two sides of one coin. Studying our world is not enough— confronting the global realities should make us want to do something about the needs we encounter. However, trying to implement change without knowledge of the world's context is shortsighted, and may do more harm than good. That is why it is so important to understand the context (how things really are) and where we can most effectively make a difference.

> We hope to motivate the reader to become a "world changer," applying this information in a way that creates a positive difference.

It is also important to understand general principles about change before jumping into action. Because a great deal of research already has been done on this topic, we attempt to summarize the main principles on how change occurs. Thus, this book first describes the "what" and "why" (the status of the world situation) and then the "how" (the ways change can be implemented). Because the majority of those who will read this book are residents of the United States, we provide additional details on American cultural assumptions, the foundational starting point for people from this nation. It is our hope to motivate the reader to become a "world changer," applying this information in a way that creates a positive difference.

The information for the book comes from many sources. The primary data were gathered from the best and most recent documents on the state of the world and its needs. The theories on change are summarized from the vast amount of literature on this topic. In addition, this material is supplemented by our actual experiences. These cross-cultural stories are of course subjective, but we feel they balance the objective information throughout the rest of the book. Both data and personal experiences are included in each chapter because there is truth in both approaches to the subjects we cover. Both are valid, bringing depth to the discussion of global issues and the process of change. In fact, they complement one another, as the stories bring a "human" element to the subjects under study, while the factual material provides the information necessary for an accurate view of the world. Together they are meant to give the reader a foundation for becoming informed and involved in global issues.

From Global Awareness to Global Change

Globalization is more than just the latest buzzword. It is an undeniable reality of ever-increasing importance today. Because there are so many different opinions on the subject of globalization and global issues, this book cannot possibly cover them all. Instead, we have chosen the topics that we think are most relevant, based on our own perspectives and experiences. All books reflect their authors' unique vision of the world, and this one is no exception. *Global Issues and Change* reflects our concern for the world, not as an end in itself, but to impel people to share that concern and to become involved in changing the world for the better. We believe the key to that action is *knowledge*——first about the global context, and then about the change process. We have seen too many well-intentioned change efforts fail because people have not researched the facts or thought through their plans.

Global Issues and Change differs from other "global issues" books in that it presents more than just the state of the world and its problems. Other sources do that but generally provide few tools for addressing global needs. Similarly, many books examine the concept of change, but rarely focus on the conditions that need to be addressed. They may cover theories and even give examples, but often do not explain *why* change is needed or *what* needs to be done. Some books give the impression that change is an academic process that can be studied and explained—not something that involves real people living in the world today.

We believe that it's not enough to just become aware of the world's condition. Everyone has a part in meeting some need. This awareness may be necessary for our long-term survival, but, more important, it is the right thing to do. The ethical dimension is also missing from many books on global issues, perhaps because the authors are concerned about taking a stand that might be unpopular in some way. This book asserts that values play a large role in any change process. Our view is that a person's values cannot be separated from that person's view of the world.

Global Issues and Change can be used in a variety of ways. As an introduction to global issues and change, we recommend reading it from chapter 1 through chapter 8. Reading it in this order maximizes the logical sequence of the material we present. However, the chapters may be read in any order, depending on what is of most interest to the reader. We include questions at the end of each chapter, which may be used for individual reflection or group discussions. These questions are not quizzes on the book's content, but rather are meant to stimulate further consideration of the issues each chapter raises. They also are meant to generate new questions, which is an excellent way to learn.

We hope *you*, the reader, gain several things from this book:

1. First, we want you to have a greater awareness of the world and its needs. We hope that you will see something unexpected, discover something you hadn't thought about before.
2. Second, we hope you will then look at the world in a different way. Gaining new facts should open your imagination to new ideas and create a wider "worldview."
3. Third, we want you to have a greater appreciation for the change process. This appreciation will provide ideas on creative ways to implement change while building on what others have contributed.
4. Fourth, we hope you will be encouraged to become involved in some positive change, to make a difference. When you are open to new possibilities, the future is exciting and full of potential!
5. Finally, we trust this book will offer ideas on how to live in a cross-cultural world. This is a new context for everyone, and it is our hope that we will help you develop a fresh perspective on how to understand yourself and others.

In summary, we wrote *Global Issues and Change* to increase our readers' global awareness, which is meant to lead to global knowledge, which in turn should lead to global concern. This foundation, we believe, can and should then lead to global *CHANGE*. The primary objective is to inform, but also to motivate. Change *is* possible, and we trust this book will be a part of that process. We live in a new world. Our next step is to find out more about that world.

Boyd Johnson, Ph.D.
John S. Johnson, Ph.D.

CHAPTER ONE

Understanding Our World

In a remote corner of the South Pacific, the inhabitants of a poor village wait patiently. American troops visited their community during World War II, and the villagers are convinced that one day a ship or plane will arrive from the West, filled with manufactured goods that will bring prosperity. The people of this village in the Pacific nation of Vanuatu are among the few remaining "cargo cults" in the region. They believe that the Westerners who once came to their islands will return, bring material riches with them, and restore selected elements of traditional culture. When co-author Boyd Johnson visited Vanuatu, he was told that this would happen soon, even though the villagers had been waiting several decades for the "cargo" to arrive.

We share this story to demonstrate the larger picture of our world today: a majority of the world's inhabitants living in poverty, seeing the wealth of other people, and wanting to find the "key" to gain some goods for themselves. Through such media outlets as movies and television programs, many of the world's poor people have been exposed to what they interpret as abundance. Naturally, they want some of this abundance. But how can they achieve this goal? Although many people are asking this question, it is a difficult question to answer.

Should all countries become like North America or Europe? Is it even possible for this to happen? If so, what changes are necessary to make it happen?

THE BIG PICTURE

Before these questions can be answered, it is important to try to understand the current world situation. By understanding world problems in context, it is possible to develop workable solutions.

Some might question why we even should concern ourselves with the world outside our borders. Perhaps they reason that we have enough problems of our own—why divert attention to global problems? This is a valid question, as the United States is not exempt from problems and should indeed address many issues. That is why this text includes an analysis of American culture (see chapter 2).

Every person lives in a culture — a culture that seems "right" to that individual.

However, it is our belief that in order to know ourselves authentically, we first should put our society in a larger setting. We need to step back and view the "bigger picture"—the global context of which our culture is only one piece. Increasingly, "international" issues touch our lives, whether we are buying foreign-made goods or worrying about foreign conflicts that may involve our military. The fact that we all live in a truly interconnected global environment should affect the way we look at the world and our place in it.

Unfortunately, most of us are not well informed about global issues. We may know a little about some other countries and even may have traveled overseas. We may know someone from another culture or have a friend who lives in a foreign country. Generally, however, we really don't know much about other nations or how these nations impact our lives. Our concerns usually are more localized, as these local issues are closer to us and may have a more direct bearing on our lives. Nonetheless, as we will point out in subsequent chapters, events that occur in far-off places can affect us greatly. These events may be economic, political, social, or environmental, but their impact today easily can be felt across national and international boundaries. A small "dispute" once confined to a distant, little-known country now can have worldwide repercussions. For this and many other reasons, all people should be better informed about global issues.

The Meaning of Culture

How do we gain a better understanding of the world? To begin with, we must first examine the concept of **culture.** By culture we mean a particular society's way of life, including the values, beliefs, and norms of behavior it passes on from one generation to the next. A *learned* system that regulates how people are to interact, culture provides rules for all members of a society to follow, helping them make sense of the world. Because this training is generally the same for all members, people in a culture know what to expect from one another. This forms a group identity, although individuals retain their personal identities as well. Everyone is part of a culture—we must be in order to survive. From the time we are born, we are taught to see the world through our culture. We view something as "normal"

> **CULTURE**
> A particular society or group's way of life, including the values, beliefs, and norms of behavior it passes on to future generations.

People learn their culture as they grow up in a particular society.

because the majority of people in our society also view it as normal. For example, most American women consider it "normal" to wear their hair uncovered. In many other countries, women consider it "normal" to wear a head covering.

As the example above demonstrates, people in other countries often have very different ideas about what is normal. To them, our ways are strange and even "wrong." Several thousand "cultures" exist around the world, and each has developed to meet the unique circumstances that groups historically have faced. Whether obtaining food, providing shelter, raising children, or maintaining security, no single culture is "right." Of course, many believe that their way of doing things is the correct way. The truth is that each culture makes sense to its members and, therefore, must be understood in its own context. This is important because while every society sees things in its own way, it also increasingly comes into contact with other groups, leading to more opportunities for misunderstanding and conflict.

As we come to understand that other cultures have different ways of seeing the world, two things should happen. First, we should realize that there are a variety of ways to view our roles and functions in life. Ours is only one approach to life. This realization hopefully will make us more open to other perspectives and more tolerant of other views. This doesn't mean that we have to adopt a new culture. However, it does mean that we can come to accept that our society is only one of several ways to organize people and their roles.

Second, as we learn to accept the intrinsic value and validity of other cultures, we then should be able to see *our own* culture more clearly. In doing this, we do not reject our society. Rather, we view it with new eyes— hopefully, more objective eyes! Seeing its positive and negative features, we begin to form ideas of how to make our society better. This even might involve incorporating or adapting features from other cultures as a way to improve our way of life.

The Diversity of Cultures

We also need to be aware of the great diversity of the world's cultures. By this we mean not just national cultures, but also **ethnic cultures**—the identities and practices that many people derive from an ethnic group and which are based on language, race, or ethnic

> **ETHNIC CULTURE**
> The identities and practices that people derive from an ethnic group.

characteristics. Sometimes ethnic groups are minorities within the larger national society. In other cases, as in Japan, the ethnic and national identities are virtually identical. The populations of most countries, however, are mixtures of ethnic groups. This can lead either to conflict and the threat of anarchy (when the groups clash) or to harmony and enrichment (when they get along). When there is conflict, it most often is due to **ethnocentrism,** the belief that one's own

> **ETHNOCENTRISM**
> The belief that one's own group is the standard by which all others should be judged.

group is the standard by which all others should be judged. People who are ethnocentric use their own group's culture as the standard or norm, judging others as wrong, deviant, or even "immoral" because they are different. These attitudes are hard to change because people are raised to think of their own ways as the "right" ways.

Ethnocentrism generally isn't an issue in a nation that is comprised of just one "culture" or that doesn't interact with other countries. But that is rare today, as virtually all nations interact in some way. Often, these ties are economic, involving the movement of goods, money, and workers across borders. Although many people only now are acknowledging this fact, the world is essentially *interdependent* economically, and has been for many years. World trade has increased dramatically in the past twenty years and international competition is a global reality. Technology has made it easier to move information, products, capital, and people around the world. This trend is escalating, making cultural interaction both commonplace and necessary.

The United States is not exempt from ethnocentrism in its view of world cultures. Many Americans believe that other countries will basically become like the United States and its distinctive culture. They believe this because the United States is a dominant force in such influential fields as business and entertainment. Those who hold this viewpoint think that a "global civilization" will develop similar to the American model. They believe that the values, culture, language, media forms, consumption patterns, democratic principles, and economic capitalism of the United States will spread to most other nations. In some respects, this is already happening. At the same time, most people have a "local identity" that comes from their own culture, and they usually want to retain this important aspect of their life. They are generally happy to adopt new technology, as this makes life easier. However, they are less likely to adopt new ways of life if these ways conflict with strongly held beliefs, religions, customs, or historical traditions.

In the next section of this chapter, we will provide an overview of various regions around the world. While it is not the intention of this text to give an in-depth analysis of the world's ever-changing dynamics, we hope to point out important facts, trends, and tenets to help the reader better understand globalization and the global issues of paramount importance today.

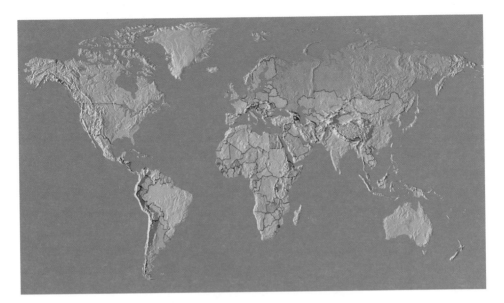

THE WORLD TODAY

Background

As in many previous centuries, the twentieth century was full of many conflicting **ideologies**. Ideologies are ideas, concepts, or goals that distinguish one group or culture from another. They are the core beliefs that form the basis of economic, political, and social decisions. These ideas can motivate individuals and nations to act in positive ways, such as helping other nations to fight disease or to grow more food. Ideologies can motivate countries to act in negative ways as well, such as invading other countries to take control. Ideologies are "models" of reality that justify individual and group acts. They are foundational to people's "worldviews." A **worldview** is the way people see the world and their place in it. Often, this conception of the world is based on a specific ideology.

By the mid-twentieth century, two major competing ideologies had emerged: communism and democratic capitalism. With the collapse of the Soviet Union, many thought that democratic ideas would

> **IDEOLOGY**
> Ideas, concepts, or goals that distinguish one group or culture from another; core beliefs.

> **WORLDVIEW**
> The way people see the world and their place in it.

spread everywhere. It hasn't been that simple. The conflict between these two main ideologies has been replaced by even more ways of seeing the world, including radical fundamentalism. This new multi-ideological reality is extremely complicated—which makes understanding it even more crucial.

This is an important place to begin a review of the global context today. Our twenty-first-century world is filled with many different ideologies that motivate individuals. Some of these ideas draw people together, like national beliefs that inspire patriotism. Others separate groups into "us" and "them," a dangerous situation in a world in which many groups have access to increasingly destructive weapons. We are living in conditions that no civilization has ever faced before. Therefore, we must identify the most significant factors and then focus on troubleshooting and resolving the implications of those factors.

To have a better understanding of the global situation today, we first will review various regions of the world, examining one country in each area to provide a basis of discussion. This will furnish the international context for a later study of the world's needs (the United States will be covered in chapter 2). As reliable information and advanced technology become available, the global picture of our world is becoming clearer. Some of this information is encouraging, such as an overall rise in literacy and life expectancy. However, some is discouraging—poverty and regional conflicts have increased worldwide. It is important to be aware of these realities as we study global issues. In every continent, there is a mixture of positive and negative factors, as the following information demonstrates.

The Middle East

The term "Middle East" has come to be used (with Europe as the point of reference) as the area east of the Mediterranean Sea across the Arabian Sea to India. Culturally, it also can include the Arab nations of North Africa. This historically has been and continues to be a crossroad, an area of great strategic importance, but also of great instability. A good deal of significant history has taken place in this region, including the formation of three of the world's major

Much of the Middle East is desert.

religions: Judaism, Christianity, and Islam. The opening of the Suez Canal in 1869 created a much shorter route from Europe to Asia, of particular importance for the development of Europe's colonies. The discovery of oil in the region increased the Middle East's significance, as Western nations developed industrial economies based on this commodity. For this reason alone, the Middle East has great geo-strategic importance.

Most of the countries in the Middle East are not genuine democracies, but instead are comprised of centrally controlled governments and economies. Of concern are the growing numbers of youth who have no job prospects. The large percentage of young males is a potential source of trouble if they are recruited for political or religious-based violence. In spite of oil wealth in certain Middle Eastern nations, most citizens in the region are poor. Oil profits have declined in many of these countries, forcing them to look for other sources of income. However, their dependency on oil makes them ill equipped to compete in the global economy. In addition, natural resources are unstable. For example, the amount of water available per capita in this region is estimated to decrease by half over the next twenty years.

Focus on Saudi Arabia

The religion of Islam was established in what is now Saudi Arabia. This nation was the birthplace of Muhammad, the man Muslims consider to be the greatest prophet. The *Al Saud* family conquered and unified the many tribes into a kingdom in 1902, and continues to rule as an absolute monarchy. Because of vast oil reserves, Saudi Arabia is an extremely wealthy nation, providing free

23

education and medical care, as well as subsidized mortgages, food, and energy for its population of 22 million. Although oil revenues have dropped in recent years, most Saudis live well compared to other Middle Eastern countries. Over four million foreigners do the jobs Saudis do not want, living under close surveillance. An extremely religious country, Saudi Arabia has very strict Muslim laws, especially for women. Females are severely restricted in their opportunities for education and work, must wear head coverings that conceal their faces, and must be accompanied in public by a male relative.

According to reliable reports, Saudi Arabia has one of the worst human rights records in the world. Religious freedom is denied to non-Muslims. Saudis who become Christians face the death penalty and may be killed by their own families. Religious police called *mutawwa* enforce the Islamic rules that govern all aspects of life.

Latin America

Colonized by Spain and Portugal, Latin America is a mixture of these two cultures plus local **indigenous** traditions. To be indigenous means to originate or occur naturally in a particular region. An area with many natural resources, Latin America has supplied much of the world's minerals, coffee, and other raw materials. It is the site of several ancient civilizations, including the Mayans, Aztecs, and Incas. These and other Latin American cultures were essentially destroyed by the colonial powers in the sixteenth and seventeenth centuries. Many local people

INDIGENOUS
Originating in or occurring naturally in a particular region.

were enslaved (along with others from Africa) to work the mines and fields. Inspired by the American and French Revolutions, many Latin American countries were involved in liberation movements in the nineteenth century. However, wealthy landowners and business elites continued to dominate the economies of Latin American nations, as they have to this day. Several countries are controlled by military dictatorships that have maintained their power through violence. A large urban underclass has no effective political representation, which creates a fertile environment for populist authoritarian leaders.

Economically, Latin America saw very high growth rates following World War II. This reduced poverty and generally led to a better standard of living for the growing middle class. But in the 1970s the region suffered several setbacks, and many nations in the region accumulated large debts they couldn't repay. Despite increased exports, Latin America as a whole has not attracted enough investment to repay its debts or effectively improve its infrastructures. Argentina has had the most problems with its economy (where half of the population now lives in poverty), and there is fear that this nation's experience will be repeated throughout the continent. Venezuela is the third largest supplier of oil to the United States, and this fact alone makes the region's stability important.

Focus on Brazil

With a population of over 165 million, Brazil is the largest country in South America. Opening its economy in recent years, foreign investments have poured in, along with foreign imports (Brazil receives one-fourth of the total imports to Latin America). It is a major trading partner of the United States, and many American businesses are investing there. In fact, the Office of the U.S.

Catholicism remains the dominant religion in Brazil.

Trade Representative estimates that by 2010 trade between the two nations may exceed U.S. trade with both Europe and Japan. Brazil is a leader in the South American trading block called *Mercosur*, which could eventually rival North America's *NAFTA*. Because of its copious natural resources and land that could sustain crops for export, Brazil has great economic potential. At the same time, however, widespread poverty, social unrest, and environmental destruction could undermine this nation's future.

East Asia

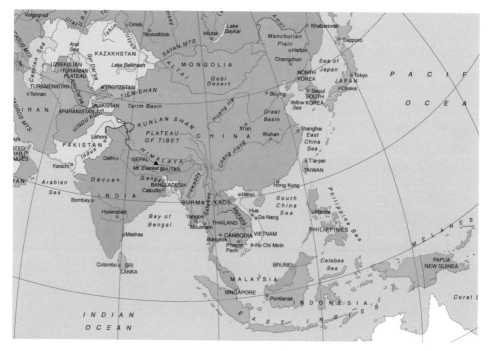

East Asia, covering the area from Japan and China to Hong Kong and Korea, is a region with a mix of ancient traditions and modern development. It is home to almost 40 percent of the world's population. Historically, the Chinese have dominated East Asia, both culturally and politically. This fact still can cause resentment in neighboring nations. Of particular importance are the social values common to this region. Most of the countries are influenced by Confucian beliefs, a two-thousand-year-old philosophy that emphasizes loyalty to authority, strong family ties, and a sense of duty. These values have an impact on almost every area of life. East Asian citizens accept powerful central governments because they generally want strong leaders and social harmony. The crime rates are low, in part because this would bring shame to the criminal's extended family. And the work ethic is strong, not only because of economic need, but also because of a sense of responsibility to others.

East Asia is a very important region economically. Despite Japan's ongoing recession, this area remains a major focus of world business. Some believe that the twenty-first century will be the "Asian Century." It is a region with vast market opportunities and low-cost labor. However, the governments have a high level of economic control and also expect companies to work for the national good. In addition, rigid social hierarchies are reflected in the business world, slowing down the capacity of companies in East Asia to respond quickly to change. Obedience to authority and a strong commitment to teamwork sometimes inhibit creativity as well. All of these factors have the potential to impact the region's economic advances.

Focus on China

Over 90 percent of China's huge population live on less than one half of its land, leading to some of the largest and most crowded cities in the world. China's population is over 1.2 billion, but the rate is slowing due to enforced

Traditional Chinese architecture gradually is being replaced with buildings in the Western style.

family planning (the "one child" policy, which gradually is being relaxed). The Chinese have traditionally referred to their country as "the Middle Kingdom" because they believe it is the center of the world. It is the world's oldest continuous civilization, surviving while other cultures have come and gone. The population is generally **homogeneous,** meaning the people are ethnically similar (although there are over fifty ethnic minority groups). Because of this, there is a feeling among the Chinese that their society is the best, and that they should be acknowledged as being better than other countries. Most Chinese practice Confucianism, Taoism, or some form of Buddhism.

> **HOMOGENEOUS**
> Of the same or similar kind. In a homogeneous population, the people are ethnically similar.

In recent history, China was ruled by emperors, with the last emperor abdicating in 1911. The Nationalist Party then ruled until 1949. After a civil war from 1945 to 1949, the communists, led by Mao Zedong (Mao Tse-tung), promised land reform and an end to poverty. Because of this, they gained support, and in 1949 the communist People's Republic of China was founded. However, the collectivist farms Mao demanded failed to bring about the prosperity he promised. Ignoring personal freedom, the PRC became essentially a *totalitarian* state, controlling all aspects of citizens' lives. Although recently admitted into the WTO (World Trade Organization), China still controls local businesses and does not allow free trade unions. The dream of a huge China market has not yet been realized for most foreign companies. Despite large problems, including budget deficits and inefficient state-owned businesses, China's economy has grown. Some estimate that it will be the world's largest economy by 2020. The real question is whether there will be political and economic reforms to allow more freedom, especially as younger leaders assume positions of power.

South Asia

Although it can be considered a geographical region, there is a great deal of cultural, political, and religious diversity in South Asia. The three main religions are Hinduism (in India), Islam (in Pakistan, Bangladesh, and Malaysia), and Buddhism (in Thailand and other countries). However, in the Philippines, the majority of the population is Christian. Much of South Asia was under British rule, but France and other European nations also had colonies here. Gradually these South Asian nations gained independence, starting with India in 1947. Mahatma Gandhi, who provided a nonviolent example for other

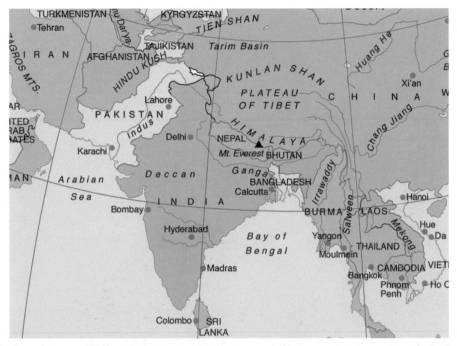

independence efforts, led this movement, providing encouragement to the other nations as they gained their political freedom.

South Asia saw some of the highest economic growth rates in the world during the 1980s, but suffered reversals in the 1990s. This was due in part to overly optimistic investments and overvalued currencies. However, there now seems to be a trend toward moderate growth based on firmer economic foundations. With an increasing number of people moving into the "middle class" (by local standards), South Asia is considered one of the more important regions for the sale of consumer goods. This will be influenced in part by these countries' governments, which range from military dictatorships (Burma), to democracies with limited freedoms (Malaysia), to democracies that have emerged after dictators were expelled (the Philippines).

Focus on India

This vast nation will soon have the largest population in the world. Throughout history India has been the site of many great civilizations, particularly the Mogul Empire. For several hundred years, India was a British colony and an important source of manufactured goods (particularly textiles). In 1947 British India achieved independence and was divided into (mainly Hindu) India and (mainly Muslim) Pakistan. These two countries have been in three

There are thousands of cultural groups in India and over 300 different languages.

wars over the disputed province of Kashmir, a sensitive issue that remains unresolved. A mix of many cultures, India has fourteen official languages.

India also has a mixed economy. Formerly socialist, it now is moving toward a free-market economy. It is a nation of extremes—boasting a number of fine universities and many educated graduates, along with hundreds of millions of people living in absolute poverty. Its social and economic development is heavily influenced by the practice of the **caste system**, a system of social class and status that is determined by birth and fixed for life. These groups range from the upper-caste Brahmins to the lowest "untouchables," who do the "unclean" work. The castes in between determine a person's place in life and often that person's choice of profession. Many feel that this ancient custom is holding India back from reaching its full potential. In addition, India is seeing a rise in Hindu fundamentalism, which wants to expel all non-Hindus from India. Many global companies are concerned because their staffs in India

> **CASTE SYSTEM**
> A system of social class and status that is determined by birth and fixed for life.

design and run their software and systems—a practice that cuts these companies' salary costs and brings an estimated $60 billion into the Indian economy.

Africa

In referring to Africa, we mean the countries south of the Sahara Desert, which extends all the way across the northern part of the continent. Some of the oldest civilizations of the world were located on this continent, although the harsh environment (particularly the lack of water) limited the development of many cultures. The later domination of European merchants and the impact of the slave trade also had a destructive impact on African cultures, causing widespread social breakdown. Selling people into slavery wrecked whole villages, tribes, and kingdoms. Gradually, Africa came under the colonial control of European nations, which continued into the mid-twentieth century.

However, political independence did not necessarily bring about a better life. True democracy has been rare, as tribal conflicts continued within nations and many dictators seized power. Although most African countries have held elections in the last ten years, there is still widespread corruption. Many African countries have remained economically dependent on foreign aid and loans, as per capita income for the region has actually decreased since the 1960s. Per capita food production also has dropped. The recent 4.5 percent economic

growth rate has not been enough to keep up with the rise in population. The top ten countries with the greatest percentage of young people in the total population are in sub-Saharan Africa. These problems have been made worse by soil erosion and the loss of fertile land to the encroaching desert. Africa as a whole must move from agricultural-based economies to other sources of income, such as manufacturing. The problem will be in deciding where these governments should spend their scarce resources: on stimulating their economies or on much-needed public services like education and health care.

Focus on South Africa

South Africa, once under British rule, became the Union of South Africa in 1910. However, only its white residents were full citizens at that time, despite being less than 10 percent of the total population. **Apartheid** (legally sanctioned racial segregation) was the law, and black South Africans had

The extensive wildlife in South Africa is a popular tourist attraction.

limited rights. Because of apartheid, international sanctions prevented trade with this nation. In 1993 apartheid finally was abolished and a new constitution established political equality. In 1994 Nelson Mandela became the first black president of South Africa. Trade sanctions were dropped the same year. Although South Africa has seen progress on its political front, the economy still is fragile, with a dependence on mining.

South Africa is a land with great natural resources, as well as a good infrastructure of communications, banking, energy, roads, ports,

APARTHEID
Legally sanctioned racial segregation.

railways, and other modern developments. There is hope that its economy will improve and more of its citizens will have opportunities for education and employment. Some even believe that South Africa could become the "gateway to Africa" if it sets a model of a market-oriented economy with value-added exports. Currently, it makes up over 45 percent of the gross domestic product of the entire continent, so its importance for Africa is clear. Exports to the United States alone are over $4.5 billion. Although South Africa's relations with its neighbors were poor during the apartheid era, this is gradually changing, and there are many opportunities for joint ventures throughout the region.

Western Europe

Europe can be divided into two parts—western and eastern—which differ in many ways. Western Europe emerged from a Hellenistic (Greek) background and flourished during the Roman Empire. Heavily influenced by the Church, both Protestant and Catholic, this region was a source of exploration and colonization of other parts of the world (often done, in part, to spread Christianity). It also was the center of the Enlightenment, which brought about new ideas in philosophy (including government), the sciences, and technology (ultimately leading to the Industrial Revolution).

Fifteen of Europe's nations have joined together to form an economic alliance called the European Union (EU). Eleven of the EU members have even begun to use a common currency, the euro. The "euro zone" will soon be the world's leading trading power, with as much economic might as the United States. The EU represents 20 percent of global trade (more than America's 16 percent), and EU exports are 25 percent greater than the United States. As other European nations meet the requirements to join the EU, it is expected that its influence will increase even more.[1] With this power, European nations are no longer accepting American economic dominance. They demonstrate their independence by such actions as banning U.S. beef that has been injected with growth hormones.

Focus on Germany

Historically, Germany has always been an important country in Europe. It has experienced almost every kind of political system: monarchy, empire, republic, dictatorship, and democratic republic. Unfortunately, it also has been the aggressor in the two World Wars—a fact that still bothers some of its neighbors. With the world's third largest economy, Germany is strategically located in central Europe in a land area the size of Montana. Divided after World War II into communist East and capitalist West, Germany was reunited in 1990—a union that has been very costly for the nation, primarily because of the outdated and inefficient economic base of the East, where communism was a huge failure.

While Germany has a capitalist economy, there is a lot of government involvement in everything from state monopolies to government ownership of company shares. Germany believes the government should play a major role as a full partner, whether in protecting domestic industries or in training workers. This has caused companies in other nations to believe German business has an unfair advantage. However, even the Germans are beginning to realize that some features of their economy, such as generous welfare benefits and job

The German emphasis on organization is evident in their efficiently run cities.

security, cannot be sustained in the competitive global business environment. Although it will never adopt American-style capitalism, Germany is changing in response to competition from many up-and-coming smaller nations that want to become global players.

Eastern Europe

Eastern Europe developed with a very different cultural background, including the Byzantine Empire and the influence of the Orthodox Church. Because the Mogul Empire ruled Russia in the thirteenth century, Russia was isolated from the benefits of the European Renaissance. Most of Eastern Europe was under the control of the Soviet Union from the end of World War II to the fall of communism in the early 1990s. Slowly these countries are now trying to become democratic and are shifting to market-based capitalistic economies. Most want to become part of the EU, mainly because of the economic advantages and development funds that will become available. But they first must build the political and economic institutions necessary for participation in the global environment. Although there were major restructuring problems in the 1990s, there is hope that many of the Eastern European nations will become stable members of the world community.

Focus on Russia

Geographically, Russia is the world's largest country and has a population of almost 145 million people. It contains many ethnic groups (18 percent of the total population) that differ in their culture, religion, and ideologies. Because of the government's commitment to atheistic communism, the Soviet regime attempted to destroy the spiritual impact of the Orthodox Church. The church, however, has been an important part of Russian life for over one thousand years. With the fall of communism, it is gradually being restored as an important part of society.

Russia is attempting to change to a capitalistic economy, but still needs a workable means of privatizing businesses and enforcing economic reforms. An unstable political system impedes economic development, particularly slowing down foreign investment. Although Russia is one of the richest countries in terms of natural resources, it doesn't utilize them in an efficient way. As in many developing nations, wealth is distributed unevenly and extreme poverty coexists with extreme wealth. As a former world power now experiencing radical transformation in every way, Russia's future is uncertain.

The Orthodox Church is still an important part of Russian culture.

This brief review of the international context is meant to be just an introduction to the interesting variety of countries that make up the global landscape in which we live. This overview provides a foundation for better understanding the next section, in which we will examine some of the main issues shaping the world today.

GLOBALIZATION

What is Globalization?

One of the most important concepts for understanding our world today is the term **globalization,** which can be defined as the increasing awareness and interaction of individuals, organizations, and businesses in an international context. This reflects the way in which the world is becoming increasingly interconnected and interdependent. Because of advances in technology, globalization also generally refers to the increasing "compression" (shortening) of distance and time,

> **GLOBALIZATION**
> The increasing awareness and interaction of individuals, organizations, and businesses in an international context.

historical limitations that are less problematic as people today can travel faster, access information, and accomplish more in a shorter amount of time. Cheaper communication by telephone, the Internet, or other means has made it easier to transfer and/or exchange information, images, and new ideas of all kinds on a daily basis. People from different societies interact more than ever before, due to immigration, business, tourism, and education.

In addition, more individuals are moving to other countries (legally or not) to find work. People are buying goods from an ever-increasing variety of sources, and financial capital can be transferred electronically and almost instantaneously. Global financial markets impact and link all national economies, so that they can no longer survive alone. Events in one part of the world (especially economic events) increasingly have implications for other nations, regardless of distance. Therefore, people are increasingly interested in global news as they begin to realize how their lives are influenced by events in distant locations. All of these factors make up the process of "globalization" as it has developed, especially in the last few decades.

The Globalization of Culture

Popular culture, in the form of movies, music, and fashion, also has become international. People are not just exposed to their own local culture today, but are experiencing different kinds of food, art, and clothing, as well. But this exposure goes to an even deeper level of culture, as people first come into contact with different ideas about political organizations, gender roles, and behavioral norms, and then to core traditions, religions, values, and ethical systems. Thus, globalization is not just about eating foods from other countries or seeing foreign films. It involves learning firsthand about different worldviews, the basic ways that people see the world and interpret their place in it. Never before in history has there been such an *awareness* of other ways of life, as well as access to other foreign cultures.

Is a Global Culture Possible?

It may seem logical that as societies interact with each other, they will create more of a "global culture," including shared foods, clothing styles, music, and other cultural characteristics. While to a certain extent this is happening, many of these changes are only "surface" changes. In other words, these cultural changes are easy to make because they involve little threat to core values or important beliefs. Standardizing the access and availability of

Many societies retain traditional ceremonies because they reinforce cultural values.

consumer goods by itself is generally welcomed in many parts of the world. However, at a deeper level, people want to retain their own cultures, including their languages, their religions, their customs, and the ways they relate to one another. Such cultural aspects as traditions and significant festivals are important and not easily changed.

Of course, globalization and the exchange of new ideas and products build on what already exists in a society. Usually people retain a part of their current culture while adopting new things. Thus, they are not just passive recipients, but pick and choose what aspects of other cultures they want to adopt. They still retain important components of their traditional cultures, especially in such areas as marriage customs and religious beliefs. These cultural aspects are linked to a society's history and identity and, therefore, do not readily change. Most people interact on a daily basis within their "local" society, which clearly will have the greatest impact on their lives. For these reasons, globalization of culture is a complex process, with different results all around the world. The concern that every culture will become the same is essentially unfounded, as the rich diversity and individuality of people seem to preclude that this will ever happen.

Is a Global Community Possible?

Regarding the possibility of a global community, consider these questions and their implications:

- Does globalization mean that common values, assumptions, and goals will emerge as people from different cultures interact? Some see this as positive, while others do not.

- Will people ever develop a common identity, or at least see themselves more as citizens of the world rather than of just one country? Some think this will never happen because people's local identities are so strong.

- Is it possible to maintain a "pure" cultural identity while being constantly influenced by other cultures? Some maintain that the mix of influences from many sources will "dilute" these identities.

- Is this change (global community) necessary for the survival of human beings in the coming century? Some believe we will not continue to exist if we are unable to share more values in common.

- Is a global community possible when there is such distance between the "haves" and the "have nots" in the world? Some feel that the wide differences in living standards will cause more resentment and despair among the poor.

- If a global community is not possible, will those who feel excluded and oppressed by the wealthy face only a future of violence and discontent? Some are very worried that this condition can lead to even more terrorism.

A few decades ago, we would not have thought to ask these questions. Today, however, they are increasingly relevant and must be answered.

Global Understanding

As people come into contact with and become more aware of other societies, they can develop a greater understanding of one another. However, as history verifies, awareness does not automatically lead to acceptance; in fact, often the opposite occurs. Cross-cultural contact can lead to increased hostility toward other groups that are different, either ethnically, religiously, or ideologically. The influences of globalization can lead to a renewed appreciation of a people's own local cultures. These influences can even cause a rise in religious fundamentalism, ethnic identification, or nationalistic political movements. People will continue to gain much of their self-identity from their local environment. To a greater or lesser extent, they also will continue to have some link to their local culture, depending on the strength of their group traditions and identity. All humans occupy a local space physically and, thus, must continue some kind of association with this cultural context. Culture has a powerful influence. At the same time, people now have the opportunity to see other ways of life. Whether they reject or accept these other cultures—and whether they realize it or not—their local societies are impacted by these cross-cultural experiences. In any event, the idea of a "pure" culture is not possible anymore.

A Marketplace of Ideas

It is important to note that globalization is not just "Westernization." Indeed, the world is being influenced by Western—particularly American—technology, culture, entertainment, economics, politics, and ideologies. It is also true that most of the features of globalization (especially free-market capitalism and mass consumerism, along with a focus on the individual) essentially developed in the West. Although American culture has become dominant due to its economic power and its control over most means of electronic communication, globalization is not just a one-way street. The United States also is being influenced by other cultures as globalization moves in all

The blend of old and new is a key feature of globalization.

directions at once. Americans (and many other Westerners) are naturally proud of their culture, but they are increasingly influenced by ideas from many other societies, particularly as immigrants come into the United States. This is a central principle of globalization: It is not just the expansion of one culture, but a multidimensional "marketplace of ideas" with a constantly changing expression of information and possibilities. Today, nothing can effectively stop this spread of ideas, as many dictators have discovered.

WORLD TRADE ORGANIZATION (WTO)
An international body that determines rules for global trade. It is comprised of most of the world's industrial nations.

People also realize that they can change certain aspects of their lives—perhaps political, economic, religious, or social—while retaining treasured parts of their current culture.

It should be clear that globalization does not primarily originate in governments. Rather, globalization stems from businesses of all kinds. They are the producers and sellers of goods and services to a broad international customer base, which in turn impacts cultures. Most industries are now oriented to reach beyond their own domestic markets. These "multinational corporations" control vast resources. Some estimate that they account for over 70 percent of global trade.[2] Many economic segments of countries around the world are now exposed to global competition, and their national governments cannot do very much to protect them from these global threats. The **World Trade Organization** (WTO), an international body comprised of most of the world's industrial nations, sets out rules for global trade, requiring nations to open their borders to foreign competition. This has taken power away from governments, who cannot set the terms of trade with their countries as in the past.

In addition, companies today can move capital and production sites all over the world, hiring whom they like, wherever they like. Because they are not limited to one country or region, these companies can select the most skilled workers from any part of the globe. Opportunities and innovations are no longer limited by geographic location. All this has been enhanced by faster and more efficient distribution systems, which move goods to markets anywhere in the world. With a reduction in trade barriers, goods are available more places than ever before.

Will this lead to a borderless world? While probably not politically, economically the mobility of goods and services across borders has completely changed how business is done. More companies are forming international alliances and joint ventures, combining their resources to gain market share and cut costs. Whether these efforts—and the spread of ideas, goods, and cultural concepts that they cause—will result in global understanding is not yet clear. But certainly it is a preferable future to one in which people don't interact or try to get along.

The Past and Future of Globalization

In many ways globalization has occurred throughout history. The early Greek, Roman, Chinese, Indian, and Mesoamerican civilizations (just to name a few) covered large territories and incorporated many smaller cultures as they expanded. But the expansion of European colonies from the sixteenth to the twentieth centuries began the process of globalization that we see today. By using military power, European nations colonized most of the rest of the world, obtaining raw materials and other wealth to enrich their economies. Of course, this was at the expense of the conquered cultures, most of which never fully recovered from political, cultural, and economic domination. The European nations justified the expansion of their "empires"—not only for economic reasons, but as a way to bring "civilization" to other people. The idea of

Many impressive buildings of the Mesoamerican cultures remain intact.

Western superiority, though not new, flourished during these centuries of expansion, with most Westerners convinced it was their duty to bring "progress" (defined as *their* way of life) to the rest of the world. This sense of a mission (and even destiny) was a powerful motivation for European expansion, a factor that continued with economic globalization in the twentieth century.

However, this process did not just happen because Westerners exploited other cultures. Local people often were involved, mainly because they profited as well.

Some nations and cultures resisted foreign influences, or were extremely selective in what they allowed "in." Most, of course, wanted to use what was beneficial while maintaining their own cultures—something that could be difficult if the "new" was seen as "better" and led to the rejection of the old culture.

In general, most people today live in what has been called a "hybrid culture," which retains traditional features while incorporating elements (both Western and non-Western features) from many other cultures. Globalization is more widespread today than during the era of European domination. It impacts more institutions, involves many more people, and influences nations from every continent. Ideas like democracy spread much faster. Conflicts, such as the one between Israel and the Palestinians, are no longer just local concerns. Ethical questions like genetic engineering cross borders. Even diseases such as AIDS are international in their impact. As we have seen, globalization is so far-reaching that it could not be stopped, even if people wanted to stop it—and most do not want that.

Opposition to Globalization

Most people favor globalization, but many argue against it. The majority of these arguments focus on the fact that economic power is being concentrated in the hands of a relatively few number of corporations. Because of their great resources, these companies can violate local labor and environmental laws, avoid taxes, control local politicians through bribes, and commit other abuses. Some fear that workers will lose their jobs as companies look for more profitable locations for their businesses. This weakens the power of unions considerably. Others argue that these companies provide employment, sell a greater variety of goods at cheaper prices, and encourage the spread of technology and training. Many poor nations naturally want to attract foreign investment, so they implement "structural adjustment programs." These programs usually eliminate subsidies, privatize state-owned industries, and reduce government spending (often on education and health—the easiest costs to cut, but the most devastating to the poorest citizens).

Many others think that because some forces oppose it, globalization has only partially succeeded. As proof, they point to the collectivist or socialist economies that still exist in various forms. Despite claims that they have "opened up" their economies, they maintain centralized government control over them. Many of these nations have state-owned industries, government subsidies, and protectionist policies that suppress competition from other nations.[3] At the same time, a number of repressive governments do not want their citizens to have access to the global market. They fear—correctly—that exposure to other nations will show their people other ways to live and the benefits of personal freedom. Some of these governments are totalitarian dictatorships, while others are religious regimes that won't tolerate alternative beliefs. These two groups share a conviction that they should have absolute power to control all aspects of life, including the economy. Therefore, they are threatened by globalization and oppose it any way they can, usually through repression. Ultimately they will fail because the forces for change and contact with other groups will only increase as the twenty-first century unfolds.

Many people have mixed feelings about the expansion of Western corporations.

What Does the Future Hold?

The future of globalization is not known. Some believe that the argument is not whether it should or should not happen—globalization is a fact of our time. Instead, the question should be: what *kind* of globalization is best? It seems that to reject the advantages of international economic integration is to glamorize poverty. (It's ironic that most of the protestors against the global economy are relatively well-off Westerners, not the truly poor from the "Two-Thirds World." The **Two-Thirds World** refers to those

TWO-THIRDS WORLD
Those countries in which the majority of the population is poor. About two-thirds of the world's countries fall into this category.

countries in which the majority of the population is poor. As the term suggests, about two-thirds of the world's countries fall into this category.)

Anything that brings more people into the world's marketplace and provides them with increased income is, overall, a positive development. But it's also true that some small nations cannot compete under the current rules imposed by the World Trade Organization. For example, they are not allowed to build their export industries by protecting their markets from foreign competition. This "protectionism" is outlawed so that there can be "free" markets. The WTO conveniently forgets that the United States, Europe, and Japan all developed their economies by imposing protectionist barriers that allowed their local industries to grow.

The important goal of globalization is to produce economic growth. However, small countries face a real danger in being linked to the world economy. Large nations can survive the radical ups and downs of the international economy, but small nations can be devastated. To illustrate, the prices for commodities (e.g., coffee, cocoa, rice, sugar, tin) produced by poor countries have fallen by more than 60 percent in the last twenty years, leaving farmers and other producers with no profits for their work. At the same time, the United States and other industrial nations have provided generous subsidies for their own farmers. This has artificially kept food prices down and made it more difficult for farmers from the developing world to export their products to these nations.

Economic growth is a primary goal of globalization, but the question remains: who will benefit the most?

Clearly, there needs to be a fairer system to spread the benefits of the global economy to more people, especially the poor. But reaching a balance between having an open economy and protecting local businesses is difficult for many countries to do. Who will create this fairer system? Governments generally want to protect their own citizens and their domestic industries, and so they usually make decisions that reflect those concerns. However, they are becoming less effective as they lose the capacity to regulate or control global businesses within their borders. Businesses want to maximize their profits and, thus, want the freedom to serve consumers everywhere. Since markets are their primary outlets, they want to be free from local or national accountability. No international body currently has the power to set up a truly fair system to satisfy everyone. Realistically, the future of globalization is up for grabs, with powerful interests competing to set the direction it will take.

Important Global Issues

Where will all of this lead? Certainly it seems that there are two forces at work: one of globalization—drawing people together, and the other of conflict—drawing people apart. Both of these forces work against each other. For example, free economic markets need stability to survive. International businesses require at minimum enough physical safety (and psychological security) to allow the movement of goods, capital, and services around the world. This is threatened by regional or ethnic conflicts. Clearly, some groups (and nations) are threatened by globalization and want to see it stopped. They are determined to keep out influences with which they disagree.

The symbol of the Cold War was the Berlin Wall, a physical division of people based on competing political-economic philosophies. If globalization today can be said to have a symbol, it is probably the Internet, the linking of people by communication, regardless of traditional barriers. The use of the Internet around the world is increasing at a phenomenal rate. Although the citizens of many countries do not have the technology they need to support the Internet (computers and cable or telephone lines), they can gain access to it through "Internet shops" that allow individuals to go on-line at a per-minute rate. In some countries, the use of international telephone lines is heavily taxed; tariffs of two to three dollars (U.S. currency) per minute may be added to a call. Other countries lack adequate international phone lines, which makes calling another country difficult, if not impossible. Communication difficulties such as these have caused the Internet to become an essential link between individuals, not only within their own countries, but also with the outside world. It will unquestionably play an even greater role in the future as people become more aware of the world and want to become more connected with it.

KEY CONCEPTS

apartheid
caste system
culture
ethnic culture
ethnocentrism
globalization
homogeneous
ideology
indigenous
Two-Thirds World
World Trade Organization (WTO)
worldview

In coming to understand globalization, those who live in the United States are beginning to realize that they can no longer live in isolation from the rest of the world. With increased interaction among the countries of the world, all of us will be required to interact with individuals from different cultural backgrounds. If we wish to be an influence in their lives, we first must know who we are and how our culture has developed over time. We explore these areas in the next chapter.

QUESTIONS FOR DISCUSSION

1. Have you experienced any other cultures firsthand? What were your impressions?

2. What geographic area do you think is the most critical for the world's future? What impact do you believe this area will have economically, socially, politically, and religiously?

3. How has your life been affected by globalization? What has changed because of this global reality?

ENDNOTES

1. Mary H. Cooper, "European Monetary Union," in *Global Issues*: *Selections from The CQ Researcher* (Washington, D.C.: CQ Press, 2001).
2. David Held and Anthony McGrew, eds., *The Global Transformations Reader*: *An Introduction to the Globalization Debate* (Malden, MA: Polity Press, 2000).
3. Brink Lindsey, *Against the Dead Hand: The Uncertain Struggle for Global Capitalism* (New York: John Wiley & Sons, Inc., 2002).

CHAPTER TWO

Understanding
Ourselves

O n a visit to the West African nation of Senegal, co-author Boyd
Johnson learned an important lesson about body language. A young
man approached him on the street and asked if Boyd would like to hire
him as his guide for the day. Boyd was surprised that the man made his request
in English, because Senegal was once a French colony and almost all visitors
are French. When asked why he didn't speak in French, the young man
immediately replied, "Oh, I knew you spoke English, because you're an
American." When asked how he knew that fact (which was true), he replied, "I
could tell from the way you walked!" It took some time to clarify what he
meant, but it soon became apparent that as a self-employed tour guide, he had
developed an extraordinary sensitivity to "body language." By watching
people's movements, he could accurately determine their nationality or country
of origin. Pressed for more details, he finally said, "Americans just walk
different from everyone else. They swing their arms and seem more confident—
like they own the world!"

This story demonstrates in an amusing way the serious fact that different
nationalities are perceived differently around the world. We may have a general

sense of this reality, but not realize its significance in our "global" environment. We may feel that national stereotypes are unfair—and yet believe them ourselves! Despite our common humanity, people *are* very different. Therefore, it is important to understand these differences and their impact on international relationships. An essential part of understanding the world is first to understand ourselves. What do we take for granted and assume is "normal"? What does our culture teach us is "right" behavior? Why do we organize our work and personal life the way we do?

> **Most people usually do not question their norms because they have been socialized to believe that their ways of thinking are the best.**

Most people usually do not question their norms because they have been socialized to believe that their ways of thinking are the best. We note in chapter 1 that the majority of people take their culture for granted, rarely questioning its values. All of us are socialized into certain behavior patterns, as well, following expected norms of how we're supposed to relate to others in our society. However, in the new global environment, we will need to examine our assumptions, especially as we encounter people from different backgrounds. Thus, we turn our attention to the specific cultural perspective that motivates what is currently the most influential nation on earth—the United States.

WHY DO WE THINK THE WAY WE DO?

Earlier, we explained that ethnocentrism is common to all people. To be ethnocentric is to use one's own culture as the standard by which to judge other societies. Ethnocentrism also can express itself as a sense of superiority over other people who have different ways of life. It puts one's culture at the center of the world, and embodies a belief (usually unspoken) that other people need to advance to *our* level of development or civilization. This is a standard belief all around the world, but is especially prevalent in the West (and, more specifically, in America), where economic wealth encourages this viewpoint. The geographic isolation of the United States in the North American continent has historically limited contact with other ways of thinking. The dominance of American business in the twentieth century also has led to a sense of superiority that in some ways has continued to the present.

Acknowledging this is important because our way of thinking forms the basis for our actions. We act from a set of assumptions about how the world is

Most values are learned within families, the primary social unit in all cultures.

organized and what behavior is acceptable and expected. This is true both in our personal lives and our public lives—our interaction with others in the workplace or in other social settings. For example, our culture defines everything from acceptable attitudes about personal ambition and gender roles, to the importance of work and the need to organize family life. But what do others think about these subjects? And—of equal importance—why do they think this way? Before we can understand the world, we must understand ourselves.

To better understand the society of the United States, we first will examine important historical eras that shaped the national culture, including key events that resulted in a new way of seeing things. We then will cover other influences on the American character and the cultural traits that resulted.

AMERICAN CULTURE:
SOME HISTORICAL FOUNDATIONS

The United States is a unique country because it has experienced a unique history. Of course, this is true of every nation, as each has experienced a different set of events that have shaped its national "character." The United States has undergone a specific series of national events, resulting in an American worldview that differs from most other countries. As we will detail, certain key circumstances combined to create a general set of characteristics that are linked in a way that is distinctly "American." This does not mean that there is just a *single* American culture. Over the years many groups have emigrated to the United States, bringing a variety of cultural practices that have either remained out of the mainstream or have been incorporated in some way. Despite many differences among the American people, they do share certain distinctive characteristics that mark them as Americans. It is this combination of characteristics that we refer to as "American" culture.

Sociologists and other observers have noted cultural patterns that are evident in everything from individual relationships to political structures, from religious customs to educational systems, and from popular entertainment to business practices. We are not saying that the characteristics highlighted in this chapter will be found only in Americans; of course, many people around the world share the same characteristics. What is unique, however, is the combination and strength of these traits, as well as the way they reinforce each other.

How did these characteristics develop? They arose from the historical circumstances surrounding an emerging nation as it progressed through a series of important milestones. Over time these beliefs were validated by experience until they became a fundamental part of the nation's worldview. Eventually they were taken for granted and passed on to each new generation. Although many events shaped the American national worldview, we will focus on five:

- the American Revolution
- the Colonial Era
- the Process of Immigration
- the Settlement of New Lands
- the Frontier Experience

The American Revolution

In the American Revolution, colonists in the New World fought for independence from the colonial authority of England. This struggle was very unique for its time, as most people in other colonies around the world—for example, Africa, Asia, and the Caribbean—either accepted their status or failed to achieve freedom. American colonists, however, were motivated by a strong belief in *freedom* and *sovereignty of the people*, as opposed to hereditary rule. Over time, they came to believe that people should be governed only with their consent, and that there was no divine right of kings to rule. Both ideas were considered to be extremely radical. Americans resisted the arbitrary and absolute authority of any monarch,

Thomas Jefferson — an American patriot.

which was an extraordinary and rare position for commoners to take. It's difficult for people today to realize what a groundbreaking idea this was for its time—a tremendous shift not only in thinking, but in behavior as well. It led the American colonists to develop an entire society based on the idea that people must be free to rule themselves, a concept that would lead to several other "American" characteristics.

The American Revolution shaped American views on freedom, especially for individuals.

The experience of successful revolution led to a strong emphasis on freedom—both individual and corporate—in American society. Americans naturally assume that freedom is a normal human characteristic. But often they fail to realize that in most societies the individual drive for freedom is usually overwhelmed by the society's demand for conformity (a topic we will discuss in more detail later). Many of those who left the "old world" to come to the United States did so because they wanted to be free from this kind of conformity. Therefore, a certain *kind* of individual often came to America— someone who wanted freedom so much that he or she was willing to leave family and homeland forever in order to get it. Although these people accepted certain forms of authority, they didn't want a strong ruler (or government) telling them what to do, a characteristic that has continued to this day. In general, the citizens of the United States today realize the need for government, but are still wary of too much government or too much centralized power.

The Colonial Era

The American Revolution was closely linked to the next historical period we will examine—the colonial era. During this time (before and after the American Revolution), people to a large extent had to rely on themselves, especially as they began to settle in the vast wilderness beyond the safety of their small settlements. The former social structures of Europe were no longer accepted or enforced, and the colonists were generally free to make their own way. This gave rise to a strong sense of **individualism,** the belief that individual needs take priority over the group's needs, and that each person is responsible for him/herself and should make decisions based on individual perceptions and needs. This characteristic is at the foundation of the American national character. Articulated by several early American leaders (particularly Benjamin Franklin and Thomas Paine), individualism is premised on the dignity of every human being.

INDIVIDUALISM

The belief that individual needs take priority over the group's needs, and that each person is responsible for him/herself, basing decisions on individual perceptions and needs.

A direct result of an individualistic worldview was a willingness to challenge authority, clearly evident in the American political system. The citizens of the United States believed in voting for their own interests, and didn't hesitate to change governments when they were dissatisfied. This belief even carried over into religion. The popular Christian faith of this time in America stressed each person's relationship with God and the responsibility of each person's duty as a Christian. The American individualistic worldview went so far as to imply that anything holding back people from living their own lives was *morally* wrong, something that most societies had never considered.

The cultural trait of individualism is expressed today in the United States in several ways. It is the main point of reference in everything from child rearing (children are taught to be self-sufficient), to education (individual achievement is stressed), to work style and decision-making (employees are responsible for their work). In fact, some have noted that self-interest—including self-expression, self-development, self-sufficiency, etc.— takes precedence in American society over most group issues, including family obligations (outside the nuclear family). This extends to the choice of a career, marriage partner, and home location—all

> In an individualistic culture like the United States, success is attributed to a person's efforts, not to the larger group or some other factor.

areas that most cultures decide collectively in some way.[1] In an individualistic culture like the United States, success is attributed to a person's efforts, not to the larger group or some other factor (like the help of ancestors). Individuals are expected to take responsibility for their actions, and this extends to their personal and professional lives. This perspective is evident from an early age, as children are expected to make decisions for themselves. Throughout their lives, Americans are given choices that would not be tolerated in many other cultures.

One example of this difference is in marriage customs. In America, the individual makes the choice of a partner. In most other cultures, the family or extended group either makes this decision or is heavily involved in the selection. In Pakistan, where co-author Boyd Johnson lived, virtually all young people (both Christian and Muslim) expected their parents to arrange their marriages. They were happy with this method because it took the pressure off them and placed it on their parents. The young people could accept or reject the choice, so their views were respected. But they did not have to go out and find a person (a major goal in the United States), allowing them to enjoy their youth. They trusted their parents to make the right choice, based on important features for any successful marriage: common background and values, shared religious beliefs, and similar life goals. They felt that love would grow during the marriage, as couples shared life together and raised their own families.

Many Americans find arranged marriages to be shocking. They disagree with the practice because it seems to violate individual freedom. But

Pakistanis—and the majority of cultures around the world—believe this decision is too important to leave to individuals, as the whole community has a stake in seeing that marriages are a success. In most places, stable families are essential because they form the only security people have. By contrast, in America individuals can make it on their own, and so they can end a marriage if it doesn't meet their needs. The American perspective of marriage demonstrates individualism and an emphasis on the self that is such a significant feature of this nation.

The Immigrant Experience

Immigration was ongoing throughout early periods of American history. The immigrants were from many nations, but they shared something important—they all had left the security of their homelands for a new home in a new country called the United States. They had cut the ties to their traditional cultures and needed to adapt to a new environment. This led in turn to a strong emphasis on **self-reliance,** which is confidence and dependence on one's own efforts and/or abilities. The immigrants found themselves in a vast new continent, often moving from the relative safety of settlements into wilderness areas. Communication systems were primitive and unreliable. Because they had brought few possessions with them, they had to make their own tools, clothing, furniture, and homes. With few opportunities to depend on others, they learned to depend on themselves, first for survival and then for building a stable, productive life.

SELF-RELIANCE
Confidence in and dependence on one's own efforts and/or abilities.

This reliance on self was tied closely to the individualism that already characterized this new country. Americans came to think that the only thing limiting people were their own efforts. This gradually created a sense that depending on others was bad, while in other cultures it was seen as not only positive but also necessary. Americans still use such expressions as "Pull yourself up by your bootstraps" and "God helps those who help themselves." In America, leaving home before marriage is a sign of maturity, while in many societies it's a sign of deviance! To this day American films and other popular entertainment present self-reliance in a positive light, focusing on "heroic" people who stand up for themselves or create something new. This often involves breaking free from some social restraints or traditions, which is a common theme in American history. Whether explorers or inventors, cowboys or mountain climbers, the self-reliant individual is still admired in America. This idea is closely linked to the

Many immigrants to America wanted their children to have more education.

dream of economic independence; thus, many Americans dream of owning their own businesses and "being their own boss." Generally, Americans accept authority, but it isn't an unquestioned acceptance (as in many societies). Americans feel that they should rely on themselves, not some authority figure.

Settlers and the Frontier

Although many immigrants stayed at first with their own ethnic groups, by the second or third generation they usually were assimilated into the wider culture. As the United States expanded, immigrants moved across the North American continent. The wide-open country seemed to offer a new opportunity for anyone who was willing to work hard. Inspired by the promise of

ACHIEVEMENT
A result gained by effort.

land, personal freedom, and economic success, many individuals became very focused on **achievement,** particularly individual achievement. To achieve is to

Settling the huge frontier forced Americans to choose practical solutions to their problems.

gain a result by effort. Unlike Europe, America did not espouse hereditary rights, a system in which a person could have others serve him because of his title or rank in society. Instead, American people worked for what they wanted and gained status through their accomplishments. In general, most immigrants to this new country were poor and couldn't expect to get something for nothing. Therefore, the majority focused on working to improve their lives. More than many others, Americans are concerned about what a person *does*. The roots of this concern in part can be found in the early American settlers.

PRAGMATIC WORLDVIEW
An attitude that emphasizes practical solutions to problems.

The settlement of the United States brought its citizens into a vast frontier, and this experience further shaped the national character. Americans felt they should expand their nation, spreading the values that they so strongly believed. In order to survive in what was often a hostile and harsh environment, the settlers had to develop a **pragmatic worldview.** This worldview reflects an attitude that emphasizes practical solutions to problems. Cut off from the institutions upon which they had depended, settlers had to produce their own food, heal their sick, educate their children, police their communities, and develop their own spiritual support. For the most part, professionals were not available to carry out these tasks, so individuals did it all themselves. Many times they were forced to improvise in order to make it through another year. Especially in the western, unsettled part of the country, new ideas and innovations were adopted quickly (and just as quickly rejected if they weren't useful). This included everything from which crops to plant to what laws were appropriate in this new environment. Clinging to old ways didn't work, so Americans became very entrepreneurial as well. To be **entrepreneurial** is to be enterprising, a characteristic of those who manage to make the most of an opportunity, even if it involves risk. The frontier became an important symbol to the people of this energetic young nation, representing new opportunities and new chances for everyone who was willing to try something different. It was up to people to take the initiative and create a better life for themselves.

> **ENTREPRENEURIAL**
> Enterprising; a trait of one who makes the most of an opportunity, even if it involves risk; the ability to create an enterprise.

In addition, the frontier experience promoted the idea that the center of control was *within* each person. Individual success or failure was not due to some external force; rather, it was due to each person. This was a critical distinction, because it put pressure on the individual to achieve as much as possible. The implications for the economic and social life of America were profound, as this nation developed what has been called a "culture of abundance." Other nations have had to struggle with a constant scarcity of resources, whereas the American experience has been completely different. The rich country the settlers inhabited provided enormous resources that seemed limitless. There was enough for everyone, leading to another cultural trait: American generosity. This was possible because early Americans believed that the accumulation of wealth by one individual didn't stop others from reaching the same goal. Of course, the frontier eventually disappeared, but that only led to the idea of exporting these ideas to other people around the world (something that other nations didn't usually appreciate). However, the impact of the frontier and the characteristics it produced are evident in the people of the United States to this day.

For the most part, Americans still have deep respect for the person who produces something, especially something new. Whether it is an idea or product, Americans consider this sort of innovation to be the key to the economic success of the United States. Americans are thus highly motivated by achievement, and are even considered by many to be a "driven" society. The need to prove oneself continues to be a motivating factor because there are few other external means of determining status. As we noted earlier, in many societies one's family or rank gives status. But from the beginning, Americans achieved this through their own efforts. Rank in America is often associated with what one possesses. Accomplishments are usually measurable. This has led to the remarkable economic advantages of the United States.

As a whole, the United States is the richest nation in history. However, much of this has come about because Americans work longer hours, take fewer vacations, and are more productive than workers in other countries. It also has been accomplished in many cases at the expense of the environment, as it seemed in the past that the country had unlimited resources. This idea of abundance—that there is enough for everyone to ensure that all succeed—is not prevalent around the world. Most nations assume that only a few can (or should) be rich. Many of these nations exist in harsh environments, leading to a "mindset of scarcity" that limits what can be accomplished. But even where there are sufficient resources, many cultures rarely have the strong drive for achievement that characterizes America.

The American Belief in Progress

These historical experiences have contributed to creating and maintaining the unique American character. Something else that sets American culture apart from other cultures is an underlying theme of optimism, the belief that things can and will be better. This sustained Americans through the difficult task of establishing and settling a new nation. Throughout this historical process, the idea of "progress" began to take shape. Of course, all people want a better life, so progress is not strictly an American idea.

> Something else that sets American culture apart from other cultures is an underlying theme of optimism, the belief that things can and will be better.

But it has perhaps its greatest expression in the people of the United States. Built on the values described above, the general consensus in America was that life could (and should) improve. Indeed, the core belief was that everything could (and should) *be* improved—usually in an economic sense. Encouraged by the expansion of the nation, the spread of education, and

The American belief in progress is demonstrated by an emphasis on technology and scientific advancement.

economic growth, most Americans developed a deep belief in progress. Progress was believed to be a result of the combined efforts of free, self-reliant, successful individuals who achieve the maximum amount of measurable accomplishment through their hard work. This conviction was one of the main features of our country, and the national experience seemed to confirm that it was the "right" view.

A "Providential" Role

The roots of the American ideal of progress can be traced back to the early settlers of the United States. Some brought strong religious convictions and believed they had a special role to play in God's providence. Soon the concept of the United States as a "redeemer nation" began, building on the idea of Americans as a "chosen" people, divinely ordained by history to be a light for all humankind. This religious motivation, along with the "frontier spirit" and its emphasis on freedom, led many Americans to believe that their way of life not only was the best, but should be a model for all other people as well. Because Americans believed progress was good and inevitable, every individual had a responsibility to improve. Being American was almost synonymous with being progressive, being open to new ideas, and not being tied to the past and old ways of doing things.[2]

Well into the twentieth century, faith in progress continued. Despite setbacks during World War I and the Great Depression, the idea of inevitable improvement continued. Americans not only wanted to improve their own society, but also the rest of the world. This had originated with the nineteenth-century idea of "manifest destiny," the belief that American ideals and ways of life should be extended to others. While at first seen as a mission to "civilize" the American frontier, it soon came to mean "the providentially assigned role of the United States to lead the world to new and better things."[3] At its best, this providential role was reflected in how the American Quakers championed freedom for the slaves. At its worst, "civilizing" the frontier meant subjugating its Native American residents and depriving them of their rights.

A Model for Others?

Although post-revolutionary America was comprised of a limited number of colonies and was not yet a world power, this young nation had many advantages over other nations: an abundance of good land and resources, a hard-working immigrant population, cheap labor, technological innovations, and a pioneer spirit. When combined, these factors led Americans to believe that their type of progress was the model for everyone else—although not all

Americans generally believe their way of life is a model of success for others.

nations agreed. It was more than a message; it was a mission, even a sacred trust given by God. Here we see the beginnings of the American desire to expand its influence, especially its economic system.

As noted by Henry May, citizens of the United States invariably used their own ideas when evaluating other societies, especially in determining others' level of "advancement."[4] The measurement of achievement was (and is) usually the *American* standard of economic improvement, and so—in the eyes of Americans—most of the rest of the world falls short. The United States is considered (by most of its citizens, past and present) to be the best example of success, a model that others should naturally follow. This has contributed to the sense of superiority that bothered (and continues to bother) other nations, especially when the United States emerged from World War II as a "superpower" and became the most powerful nation after the collapse of the Soviet Union in the 1990s. Because of this development, the United States is now in a special position to impact the rest of the world.

AMERICAN CULTURE: IMPORTANT CULTURAL TRAITS

Defining "American"

It is evident that over time Americans have developed many characteristics that distinguish them from the people of other countries and societies around the world. But what is it that makes someone distinctly American? "Being a citizen of the United States" certainly isn't the answer we're looking for. That may be a legal definition, but we're interested in the *cultural* characteristics that set Americans apart. Although any traits we define here can be found in other parts of the world, certain characteristics seem particularly prevalent among Americans. The unique combination of these characteristics is of special interest. Although we acknowledged previously the many variations among the different citizens of the United States, we will take the liberty of referring to "American" culture as the characteristics that are most common to this group. We will focus on six primary cultural traits: competitiveness, equality, concern with time, focus on the future, risk-taking, and patterns of decision-making.[5]

A Competitive Spirit

Competition not only is an accepted part of American culture, it is the primary means by which people are motivated. In fact, this characteristic is often considered to be a key to understanding Americans. It is instilled early, at home and then at school, with rewards for being the best. From this beginning, a competitive spirit naturally carries over from school and sports to the business world. In business, competition is considered to be the most effective way to produce better products and services. Americans view competition as a healthy part of society, even in leisure activities, as it is believed to bring out the best in people, allowing them to reach their full potential. As a nation, America strives to be "number one," whether in Olympic competition, space exploration, or as a military might. Americans have great respect for "winners" and anyone who succeeds—especially if that winner has overcome great adversity or obstacles. In many other collective cultures, the idea of competition is unpopular because it rewards *individuals*, thus causing a possible *disruption* of the group. When these cultures allow competition, it is usually between groups, not individuals.

Competition expresses itself in all areas of American culture. At an early age, children are introduced to games in which there are clear winners and losers—

Competition is considered a "normal" part of American life, especially in sports.

something that isn't done in all societies. Children in the United States quickly learn that the way to succeed is to "outdo" others. To excel in some activity is applauded and encouraged, whereas in many cultures self-promotion at the expense of the group is thought to be wrong or even deviant. Competition is especially evident in American business, which is expected to involve a struggle to overcome competitors.

"All Men Are Created Equal"

As an expression of American individualism, Americans also believe in *equality,* or at least the principle of equal opportunity. They consider themselves generally to be of the same status and stature as others. Therefore, they prefer not to have rigid hierarchies, either socially or in the workplace (except for the military or similarly structured organizations). This can be traced back to

> **UPWARD MOBILITY**
> The ability to rise to a higher social or economic position.

the frontier experience and the widespread preference to base social standing on achievement alone. This is also the time the concept of "upward mobility" took root in the American culture. **Upward mobility** is the belief that all people

In the United States, education is viewed as a means of upward mobility.

should be given the opportunity to improve their lives by rising to a higher social or economic position. Yet despite the implications of this mobility, Americans prefer to downplay status differences when they relate to one another, and like to believe that everyone has an equal say. Promotion to leadership positions is based (at least in theory) on accomplishment and ability, not on someone's family, social standing, or age. Calling attention to one's higher position is generally considered arrogant, rude, or even a sign of that person's insecurity. Authority in the workplace is accepted, but it is thought best to use it infrequently. And while Americans respect superiors, over the past few decades they have come to feel they can question the decisions of those in authority over them. They also don't give the deference that is expected in hierarchical societies. In fact, some other cultures view Americans as less sophisticated because the "proper" respect is not given to those in higher positions.

This idea of equality is best demonstrated in the way Americans organize their social lives. For the most part, people in the United States are uncomfortable with the idea of "class"—ranking individuals by their social position. Although there are distinctions between groups, it is not as important as it is in other countries and where it exists, it is not as rigid. In the United States, distinctions are usually made by wealth, which can be earned. In one generation, a person can move to a higher social standing because of the money that individual earns. But this status is not hereditary; that is, it is not passed on because of a family's name. Thus, in one generation, someone also can move down the social ladder. In general, however, Americans believe strongly in the concept of equality. They attempt to underscore this concept through such institutions as public education and the legal system (where in theory everyone has the same rights). Children are taught that "all men are created equal," an important part of the national ideology. This belief is reinforced by popular stories that demonstrate how a person can be born into poverty but later succeed through hard work and opportunities available equally to all citizens of the country.

Obsessed with Time

Another distinctive American cultural trait is a concern (some would say obsession) with *time*. As a forward-looking nation, the United States throughout its history has produced citizens that value time and productivity. Settlers of this new country took on the enormous task of building a new society. They worked with determination and urgency. Americans have retained this sense of urgency up to the present time. Some cultures view time as cyclical, a concept that sees the past as a part of the present in a very real way. The future also merges with the present and is not distinctly separate, as it is for Americans. A cyclical worldview often accepts certain patterns as changeless and ever repeating themselves.

CHART 2.1			
CONCEPTS OF LATENESS			
	Lateness excused	Tension	Hostility
Yapese	2 hours	3 hours	4 hours
Latin American	1/2 hour	1 hour	2 hours
North American	5 minutes	15 minutes	1/2 hour

Source: Sherwood G. Lingenfelter and Marvin K. Mayers, *Ministering Cross-Culturally: An Incarnational Model for Personal Relationships* (Grand Rapids: Baker Book House, 1986), 39.

Americans and most Western nations see time as linear. It has a distinct past, present, and a future. It moves forward and is closely tied to the idea of progress, with the belief that improvement is possible as individuals use present opportunities to change the future. Americans usually view time as something to be *used*, like any other resource, and therefore are upset when it is "wasted"—an idea that many other cultures find amusing. They also want things done immediately, which is the reason for the popularity of "fast food," fax machines, credit card payments, overnight courier mail, and instant Internet messages. Related to this is the rapid pace Americans are expected to keep.

Visitors to the United States frequently remark on how everyone in America seems to be continually busy at work or play, trying to fit so much into each day. Americans expect entertainment and sporting events to start on time and follow set schedules. In the business world, productivity and speed are such major concerns that a tangent industry of time management is a hugely profitable enterprise. Most workers know that they are required to be on time and to put in a set number of hours each week (and most work more). Personal planners are everywhere and almost everyone wears a watch. Punctuality is considered essential. It is unacceptable to be late for meetings or parties unless there is a good reason, and Americans are personally offended if they're kept waiting beyond what they consider an acceptable point.

What do other cultures regard as an "acceptable" waiting period? Chart 2.1 compares the American view of waiting to the views of some other cultures.

In rushing through each day, packing it as full as they can, many Americans miss out on what is truly important. Focused on accomplishing more in less time, they neglect the relationships that are a major part of human satisfaction and enjoyment of life. This erosion of personal relationships can significantly lower the quality of life.

Future Oriented

Closely related to the cultural trait of time is the American *focus on the future*. Generally, cultures can be categorized by whether their primary orientation is toward the past, the present, or the future. In some societies the past is used as a guide for the present, but in the United States the past is often seen as irrelevant or even as an obstruction to progress. Present-oriented societies, such as some in Latin America and southern Europe, believe that each day should be enjoyed for the opportunities it presents. Their focus is on immediate issues, while Americans in general are willing to give up short-term pleasure for long-term goals. The United States overall has been more concerned about what *can be* instead of what *has been*. A generally optimistic people, Americans think that their actions can achieve the results they want and that they can control how things will turn out. Very few societies share these beliefs. Americans also think that their efforts will be rewarded, necessitating the careful setting of goals. This provides a strong motivation for improvement and also a sense of confidence (which others sometimes see as arrogance). Many other cultures have a more fatalistic mind-set, resulting in an attitude of acceptance when goals are not met as planned.

America's future focus is evident in the emphasis on planning. Americans are encouraged to set one, five, and even ten-year "strategic" plans for their lives, mapping out their goals with great detail. The national tendency is to emphasize the "new" as "better." Things that are old—whether objects or ideas—are often dismissed as out-of-date and, therefore, irrelevant. This is particularly noticeable in advertising, where "new and improved" is applied to every product. Americans want the latest technology, the latest automobile, and the latest home entertainment system. They rarely look to the past for direction; in fact, "old fashioned" is usually applied in a negative sense. Americans *expect* things to change and demand new products to replace outdated ones (even if the outdated items still work). They are willing to throw out "old" ideas as well, replacing them with new ones that adapt better to a changing environment. This is especially true in business, where innovation is the key to capitalist growth.

Open to Risks

The above cultural traits are linked to the American propensity for *risk-taking*. The roots of this can be found historically in the type of individual who was willing to give up familiar surroundings and make a new life in a strange country. This characteristic was and continues to be strong in the world of commerce, with a strong emphasis on entrepreneurial activities. Most people in the United States continue to respect those who take risks and applaud those who are willing to try something different, whether in business or in other professions.

As a culture, Americans like to try new products, so much so that they feel they achieve "status" if they're the first to buy something new. They are very supportive of innovations in many areas of their society, including education, social programs, medical research, and the space program. Americans are open to new experiences, as well. This goes beyond the friendly competition of "who can outdo whom" during summer vacation. The prevalence of self-help books and "pop" psychology gurus demonstrates that Americans are willing to take risks in changing their ways of thinking. This involves risks in order to "move up" in life. These risks can mean relocating because of work opportunities, changing jobs, upgrading skills through additional education, or branching out into independent

The space program is an example of American risk-taking.

business. Living in a country where "anything is possible," many Americans learn to accept and even enjoy the uncertainties (what they see as challenges) of a changing future, tolerating them in order to have a better life.

However, risk-taking finds its greatest outlet in business, where innovative products and services serve as the lifeblood of the economy. The dangers of failure are always present, but American companies thrive on this challenge. While some foreign competitors are reluctant to gamble on untried methods, American business people are usually willing to move into "uncharted waters," making themselves vulnerable in order to succeed. Sometimes this risk-taking involves branching into new areas, especially in developing new technologies such as computer software. It's no accident that so many inventions have originated with Americans.

> **Most people in the United States continue to respect those who take risks and applaud those who are willing to try something different.**

Decisively Individualistic

Finally, American *decision making* tends to follow the same pattern as other aspects of the American culture. It is:

- rapid (time conscious)
- direct (to the point)
- future oriented (concerned with results)

The emphasis is on goal setting and measurable results. In contrast to the collective approach of many other societies, individuals themselves make personal decisions in America. This places the responsibility for decisions on each person—typical for a culture high in individualism. We explained earlier in this chapter that all of this was necessary as Americans originally developed their country without traditional leaders or a strong central authority like a king. Most societies around the world have well-established systems for decision making that go back for centuries or more. However, in the United States the vast distances and an independent spirit led to a focus on the individual. Where it was necessary for a group to decide something, the majority's opinion prevailed because it expressed the consensus of the most individuals. This has remained an American characteristic that is consistent with the nation's preference for action.

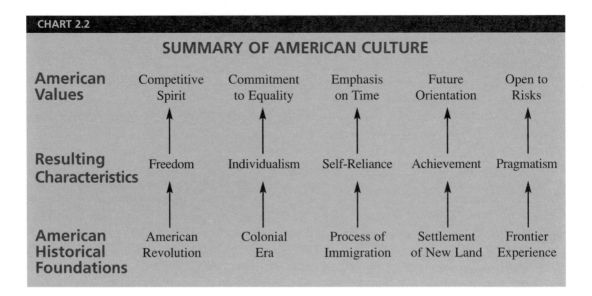

CHART 2.2

SUMMARY OF AMERICAN CULTURE

American Values	Competitive Spirit	Commitment to Equality	Emphasis on Time	Future Orientation	Open to Risks
Resulting Characteristics	Freedom	Individualism	Self-Reliance	Achievement	Pragmatism
American Historical Foundations	American Revolution	Colonial Era	Process of Immigration	Settlement of New Land	Frontier Experience

This characteristic is evident in the way Americans raise their children. In our discussion of individualism, we noted that American children are given responsibility for their decisions at a relatively early age. In many collectivist societies, however, the family makes most of the decisions for the children—including everything from the children's education and future professions to their marriage partners. Families in the United States would never tolerate this! Americans are too used to making decisions for themselves and either don't want to give up their freedom or are too impatient to take the time that a group decision involves. Perhaps more significant to American parents, making most of their children's decisions instead of letting them decide for themselves would mean not allowing these children to take risks, which is so important to personal development (in America). Overall, Americans will talk to others, ask for advice, and consider what others have written or done, but they ultimately want to decide things for themselves.

Chart 2.2 summarizes the characteristics described in this section. It provides an overview of the main features of the material we have covered, and how these traits are distinctively expressed in American society. With this foundation, we now will briefly examine some views of American culture, from within and from outside the country.

AMERICAN CULTURE

How Americans See Themselves

It is evident that America's unique history has had a large part in forming the cultural traits that distinguish this country from others around the world. These historical foundations and cultural traits have led to particular assumptions about human behavior—primarily that they take for granted "their" perspective and way of doing things and think they are true for all people. Over time, Americans—like the people of most countries—came to think of their experiences as the norm for all societies. This ethnocentric perspective translates into the belief that "our way" is best. The position of the United States as a world power since World War II has contributed to this sense that its culture must be the "right" way to live. As a military superpower, it has been able to defend its interests globally. As an economic leader, it has been able to market its products to almost every part of the world. The United States has been particularly successful in exporting its popular culture (especially films and music), reinforcing the idea that the American way of life must be best.

Because of this success, Americans have developed blind spots regarding their culture, often assuming that other cultures are either like them or should be. Most people naturally use their own culture as the "yardstick" to measure others—and many use economic criteria. But Americans especially judge others by external factors, such as income, housing standards, or material possessions. They assume that all people can advance if they "just work hard enough" and apply themselves to achieve their goals. Because of this emphasis on achievement and material possessions, they often consider other societies "inferior" to the United States.

Wealth is often used as a measure of "success" in the United States.

A Privileged "Edge"

What the citizens of the United States often forget, however, are the very unique circumstances that created their country and the advantages they have had throughout their history. To list just a few:

- Their living standards have improved over most other countries, so that they have one of the highest standards of living in the world today.

- They have not had to live under a dictator or a repressive government.

- They have not been invaded or colonized by a foreign power (although such events as Pearl Harbor, the Cuban Missile Crisis, and the 9/11 attacks impressed the very real threat of these realities upon their collective conscience).

- They have had more freedom than any other people in history.

- They have benefited from the energy of highly motivated immigrants.

- They have more access to college education than any other nation (with over half of bachelor and master's degrees awarded to women).

Ian Vásquez said this about America's wealth: "It is amazing but true that more financial wealth has been generated in the United States over the past 50 years than was created in all the rest of the world in all the centuries before 1950."[6] That statement alone speaks volumes. From an economic perspective, the United States as a whole definitely has had advantages that no other country can match.

A Shift in Perspective

Is a wealthy society necessarily a good society? Other cultures define "good society" in other ways, using other measurements besides wealth or material progress to determine whether a society is doing the "right" things. In particular, they emphasize such factors as family life and social relationships. They see these issues in a different light, with less concern for individual success. In some ways Americans are also starting to question whether their norms are the right ones. They are becoming more concerned about their "quality of life" rather than just their potential "quantity" (having more) in life. Although they

> In America, balancing individual goals and group needs continues to be a challenge.

still prize independence, they realize that this may inhibit close support from others. And while they still believe in self-reliance, they realize that this may separate them from the community that they need. This is true even in the business world, where "networking" has become more than just a buzzword.

The idea of progress still motivates many Americans, but there has been some shifting away from the optimism that historically characterized American society. This has taken on particular significance as Americans have become more aware of the problems in their society, including the number of people in poverty (especially children) and the growing gap between the rich and the poor. This has led to an awareness of past injustices and concerted efforts to both inform the American public and rectify these grievances. Two such efforts in the past fifty years have been the Civil Rights movement (and resulting legislation) and reparation to American citizens of Japanese descent who were interned during World War II.

Some wonder if the materialism of American culture has gone too far, eroding spiritual values in a single-minded quest for money. Family life also seems to have suffered, with negative results from the large number of divorces and illegitimate births. American children often don't have the security or guidance they need for healthy development.

In the American political world, it is common today for special interests to dominate elections and the legislative process, ignoring the good of the larger community. While the ideal of personal autonomy is still strong, some Americans are asking if this characteristic has taken something away from the commitment to community that once was an important part of the national culture. Thus, balancing individual goals and group needs continues to be a challenge.

Some question whether the "American Dream" is possible, or even desirable.

Other factors have also influenced Americans' changing views about their country. Among these are the major population shifts away from rural areas to urban centers, with people today moving to new areas at an unprecedented rate. This most often involves leaving family and "hometowns." The mobility of American citizens has led to an isolation from others that is unique in history (even for this self-reliant people), particularly because they often develop a sense of identity from their accomplishments and not from family or community traditions. Generally, there is a weakening of social connections and less participation in communities.[7] Added to this are the demographic changes from immigration. This has brought large numbers of people to the United States who have very different cultures and varying assumptions about what it means to be an "American." (One significant development, for example, is that currently there are almost as many Muslims [5.5 million] as Jews [5.9 million] in the United States). Therefore, the perspective Americans have of themselves and their nation is changing, and it raises the question of what the country will be like in twenty-five, fifty, or one hundred years.

How Others See America

Americans can learn a great deal about themselves by reviewing how other people view American culture. Because outsiders have different expectations, they are not used to seeing things with American assumptions. They will question American cultural practices, whereas Americans will unconsciously accept their ways as "normal." Outsiders can see what Americans may not, and also can find new meanings in things that insiders take for granted. This cultural "distance" makes their insights very useful for American society.

MERITOCRACY
The advancement of people due to achievement, not social background or privilege.

One feature some foreigners notice is the "mental break" that Americans have made from the "old ways." In some countries to which immigrants move, the newcomers keep their culture. In the United States, immigrants often quickly embrace their new culture. This has resulted in a "culture of mixing" in which newcomers are free to become almost anyone they want.[8] Many foreigners are impressed with American **meritocracy**—the advancement of people due to their achievement, not to their social background. Meritocracy assumes that if individuals have equal opportunities, the most skilled or talented ones will be able to make a full contribution. However, these same foreigners are not as happy with the related American belief that success then is up to the individual; therefore, failure is also the fault of the individual. As they see it, this appears to put too much stress on the individual, when several other factors may be responsible for what happens. Overall, however, outsiders are impressed with the attribute of American optimism. More than any other nation, this is a trait that is especially characteristic of America.[9]

These are not new perceptions about Americans. Even in the eighteenth century, observers recorded that not only did the citizens of the United States have more personal initiative and self-reliance than Europeans, they also were not concerned with social rank. They were seen as rational individuals, focused on their own well-being and self-interest. Already the expression of a competitive spirit was evident, especially in the business world where each person was free to work for himself.[10] A century ago, one source recorded that Europeans felt Americans were only motivated by the desire to make money, and that they overemphasized individual freedom at the expense of the good of the community.[11] It appears that these features have remained for well over two hundred years, seemingly an ongoing part of the American character.

Trained to Observe

In our own time, it is interesting to see the impressions that outsiders have of Americans. In *Distant Mirrors: America as a Foreign Culture*, authors Phillip R. DeVita and James D. Armstrong survey fourteen foreign social scientists who have lived in the United States and who have a unique perspective given their training in observation.[12] As we review three of these social scientists and a fourth immigrant to the United States, we will relate their experiences to pertinent American cultural traits.

Poranee: Only So Far

Poranee is from Thailand. She notes that Americans at first seem quite open and friendly, but this only goes so far. They value their privacy more than Thais do, and so American social relationships in general seem somewhat superficial. She thinks this is related to the strong emphasis on independence in the United States, where children are taught to become economically and emotionally self-reliant from an early age. By contrast, in Thailand individuals stay within a much closer family network their entire lives, and usually don't leave home to make their own way. They see more value in being a good family member than in personal achievement or financial success—both of which are very significant to Americans. Families are indeed important in the United States, she notes, but not to the same extent as in Thailand. Poranee's perspective seems to reflect a focus on American *individualism*.

Janusz: Friendly Arrogance

Janusz, a Pole, comments on Americans' "friendly arrogance." By this he means that while the majority of people in the United States are well meaning and generally like people from other countries, they know very little about them. Because of this they are very ethnocentric, believing that their way of life is the best. This attitude, he believes, is caused first by the American educational system, which teaches very little about other nations or cultures. World history isn't a priority in American schools, so few students know how their culture differs from other cultures. The second reason for American ethnocentrism, Janusz says, is **parochialism,** which means to have a narrow or restricted view of things. The United States itself is so large that many of its residents feel they really don't need to learn anything about foreign places. Finally, Janusz notes that the American mass media usually focuses on local concerns or treats the world as just an extension of America. By this he means that the media in general is interested in events within the borders of the United States, or in foreign events that impact the United States. Because of this, the people of the United States are often unaware of how interdependent their nation is with the rest of the world's nations. In this respect, Janusz seems to focus on American *self-reliance*.

> **PAROCHIALISM**
> Limited in range or scope; a restricted view of the world; provincial, narrow-minded.

Amparo: On a First-Name Basis

From the Philippines, Amparo wasn't prepared for the casual way Americans addressed older people and others in positions of authority. She was particularly surprised by the use of first names, something that would never be done in the Philippines. In her society, there is a very strong value placed on obedience to authority. Respect is shown by the use of specific terms that are the equivalent of "sir" and "ma'am." These terms *must* be used; not to use them is considered rude. Americans, on the other hand, rarely use these kinds of terms (except in some regions where traditions are strong), considering them outdated and unnecessary. Amparo felt she was caught between two cultures as she raised a daughter in the United States—a common experience of immigrants who want to hold onto customs from their home country. But which way is "best"? In this case, Amparo's focus on the issue of respect and authority reveals another American characteristic, the desire for *equality*.

Anna: The Christian Mix

A recent interview with Anna from Ukraine reveals yet another view of American culture. After living in the United States for a year and a half, she has especially noted how optimistic Americans are about the future and how much they emphasize overcoming discomfort and difficulties. However, this effort often just addresses immediate difficulties, rather than looking for

In most cultures, older people are given great respect.

long-term solutions that require sacrifice. Anna also thinks that American Christians have incorporated many of these values, viewing success as a good thing. They see God's grace in the attainment of material comforts, and believe that problems should be overcome because God is pleased when people enjoy their lives. Anna notes that this is different from other Christian traditions that emphasize a detachment from the world; i.e., Christians of other cultures draw more of a line between themselves and the secular society in which they live. Americans seem more comfortable mixing secular and Christian ideas, especially in the economic realm. Anna's focus seems to stress the American cultural trait of *achievement*.

Summary

In attempting to understand the United States as a nation in relation to the other nations of the world, this chapter has just highlighted the key characteristics of American culture. Still, it is easy to ascertain that Americans are a unique people. They are unique in their history, which is much shorter than that of China or Europe. They take pride in how they have become who they are, how their culture has developed, and how they have progressed economically. Also evident is that occasionally the advantages of history can blind a group, including Americans. These ethnocentric blinders can cause them to imagine that other nations of the world either are experiencing the same level of prosperity or have the ability to achieve prosperity—if they want it badly enough. Of course, this is not true. In chapter 3, we will expand our understanding of the world to include the complexity of the global situation.

KEY CONCEPTS

achievement
entrepreneurial
individualism
meritocracy
parochialism
pragmatic worldview
self-reliance
upward mobility

QUESTIONS FOR DISCUSSION

1. What American characteristic do you feel is most important? Why do you believe this?

2. Do you think the idea of progress is still a major force in American culture? If not, what has changed?

3. Do you agree with the impressions of social scientists and others in the previous section? Do you think outsiders have an accurate view of Americans?

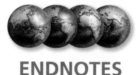

ENDNOTES

1. Francis L. K. Hsu, *The Study of Literate Civilizations* (New York: Holt, Rinehart and Winston, 1969).
2. Ibid., 81.
3. Anders Stephanson, *Manifest Destiny: American Expansionism and the Empire of Right* (New York: Hill and Wang, 1995).
4. Henry May, *The End of American Innocence: A Study of the First Years of Our Time 1912–1917* (New York: Alfred Knopf, 1959), 148.
5. Several of these points are adapted from Edward C. Stewart and Milton J. Bennett, *American Cultural Patterns: A Cross-Cultural Perspective*, rev. ed. (Yarmouth, ME: Intercultural Press, Inc., 1991).
6. Ian Vásquez, ed., *Global Fortune: The Stumble and Rise of World Capitalism* (Washington, D.C.: Cato Institute, 2000).
7. Robert Bellah, ed. *Habits of the Heart: Individualism and Commitment in American Life*, 2d ed. (Berkeley: University of California Press, 1996).
8. Jean Baudrillard, *America*, trans. Chris Turner (London: Verso, 1989), 82.
9. Seymour M. Lipset, *American Exceptionalism: A Double-Edged Sword* (New York: W. W. Norton & Company, 1996).
10. Bellah, *Habits of the Heart*, 35-36.
11. Hugo Munsterberg, *American Traits: From the Point of View of a German* (New York: Houghton, Mifflin, & Co., 1901; reprint, London: Kennikat Press, 1971.)
12. Phillip R. DeVita and James D. Armstrong, *Distant Mirrors: America as a Foreign Culture* (Belmont, CA: Wadsworth Publishing Company, 1993).

CHAPTER THREE

Understanding
the World's Needs

W hile visiting a village in India, co-author Boyd Johnson was invited into one of the simple homes. There he discovered that his hosts' young daughter had a high fever. Since Boyd always carries a small "first aid" kit with him when he travels, he gave some aspirin to the parents of the sick girl. He was struck by the look of gratitude on their faces and by their tears of joy. Something that most Westerners take for granted and to which they have ready access—simple, inexpensive aspirin—was beyond the reach of this poverty-stricken family. Boyd has never forgotten that experience, seeing in this family's plight the basic needs of so many in the world today.

NOT JUST "OUT THERE"

In chapter 1, we considered what it means to be a "world changer," how we need to understand first the world and then the process of change. One of the most important aspects of understanding our context is to examine what challenges we face. These challenges may take many forms, but all of us in one

This boy lives with other abandoned children at a railway station in India.

way or another must confront them. At first glance, some of these issues may seem distant or unrelated to our reality. The globalization process described in chapter 1 should make clear that what at first seems irrelevant can quickly take on significance. Whether it is poverty that results in social unrest, environmental problems that cross national and international boundaries, or a rapidly expanding population that threatens global resources, each of these realities has the potential to affect all of us dramatically. For this reason, we must learn more about how to respond to these worldwide needs.

Globalization has made the problems "out there" *our* problems. The "shrinking" of the world has made the needs of the earth's population everyone's concern. Nations no longer can live in isolation, separated from one another. Is this a negative development in the history of humanity? Not at all! Rather than harbor fear and confusion, we should see this world-changing shift as a positive and unique opportunity in human history.

With that in mind, this chapter will examine five major global issues:

- Poverty
- the Environment
- Population
- Politics
- Conflict and Security

We then will review various proposals on how to solve these global problems, concluding with some theories of how to bring "development" to the poor. While we cannot possibly offer a comprehensive analysis of global problems, we hope that our overview will spur further study and possible solutions to the challenges ahead.

Confronting the World's Challenges

As we begin the twenty-first century, what are the most urgent global challenges? We have identified some of these global concerns in the preceding section and will explore them in more detail later in this chapter. The very fact that we reside on this planet makes us global citizens. Thus, it is our responsibility to be aware of how we impact one another. One reason for concern, of course, is that we are "connected" to other people in other countries to a greater extent than at any other time in history. It is important to be informed of their struggles and to develop ways to help overcome these problems. To do this, we first need to review the general context of the Two-Thirds World, the developing nations where most people live and where the needs are the greatest.

> The very fact that we reside on this planet makes us global citizens.

Putting the Two-Thirds World in Context

For the last four hundred years, Western nations have dominated the world economy. This is due primarily to the Industrial Revolution and the resulting availability of superior technology. The application of science to all areas of production furthered Western development at the same time that European nations extended their colonies globally in order to access cheap raw materials and labor. The West sustained its economic advantage through a combination of innovation, entrepreneurial expertise, and the use of military advantage to maintain its top position in the global economy. Over time, non-Western nations naturally wanted to "catch up" and share in the prosperity, especially twentieth-century nations.

The majority of the earth's population lives in what we refer to as the Two-Thirds World, the areas outside North America, Europe, and the other economically "developed" regions of the world. Earlier we defined the Two-Thirds World as those countries in which the majority of the population is poor and, as the term suggests, two-thirds of the world's countries fall into this category. These countries are of great importance because in many ways their future will determine what happens to the human race. Through much of the twentieth century, most of these nations struggled under colonialism, dictatorships, and communist regimes, and were considered peripheral to the world's economy. But by the end of the century, major changes had occurred, among them the end of colonialism and the fall of communism. Democracy became possible because populations were better educated and desired a participatory role in their futures. Globalization exposed them to other ways of life, and naturally they wanted the same freedoms that other nations were experiencing. They saw neighboring countries attract capital, apply technology, and foster economic growth, and they wanted the same opportunities.

LDCs
An acronym for less developed countries.

However, achieving these goals has proven to be difficult. One of the main problems is deep poverty, which we will discuss below. National markets and financial security are generally improbable without the existence of a stable middle class. Thus, many poor countries already are at a disadvantage as they try

Jobs are scarce in many poor countries of the world.

to develop a competitive edge in areas best suited to their economic strengths. In addition, most of these less developed countries (**LDCs**) remain dependent on richer nations, working to pay off loans they have used for economic survival. They also are slowly getting rid of ideologies that have proven to hold back development, such as communism and various kinds of dictatorships. As if that weren't enough to challenge the Two-Thirds World, they have to battle the other problems we will look at in this chapter: environmental destruction, exploding populations, uncertain political situations, and the resulting conflicts and instability from the clash of these global challenges. Currently, both political and economic changes are needed so that these nations can become "emerging" economies, capable of raising the living standards of their people.

Because the Two-Thirds World cannot compete globally, many have opened their borders to over 10,000 multinational corporations (**MNCs**). In chapter 1, we noted that globalization has created new goods and services for the world market, and MNCs are using materials and labor from all over the globe to satisfy their global customers. As labor costs in developed countries like the United States, Japan, and Europe have increased, multinational corporations are moving their production facilities to cheaper sites. They offer much-needed jobs to workers in poor countries, where labor costs are low. Although some criticize MNCs for paying low wages, others believe they help developing nations on the first step to overcoming poverty. As such, most countries offer incentives for these companies to set up operations, such as tax breaks, reduced export duties, and low-cost leases, to name a few. Eventually, most of these nations will see wages rise over time, assisting the local economy even if some MNCs move on to cheaper locations.

MNCs
An acroynm for multinational corporations.

As the number of consumers in Western countries stabilizes or decreases (due to aging populations), multinational corporations also continually look for new markets to increase sales. They particularly anticipate future customers from the youth in developing nations, especially as this young population gains more income. MNCs in many of these countries are laying the groundwork now for future sales, hoping that these individuals will buy their products as their purchasing power increases. In fact, many Western companies already sell more of their products or services in the developing world than in their home countries. Whether this can become a global reality, however, hinges on the enormous problem of poverty.

GLOBAL POVERTY

Poverty is a way of life for much of the world. The situation for many people, especially children, is grim. Gordon Brown explains:

> Every <u>day</u> this year, 30,000 children will lose the fight they are waging for life. Seven million children will perish before reaching their first birthday, and over ten million will die before the age of five. Of those children winning their fight for survival, 113 million have no access to primary education, 60% of them girls. Millions more do not complete the five years of schooling needed to develop the basic literacy and math skills that would last them a lifetime. This is the face of global poverty today.[1]

Why do we need to know or care about this grim face of poverty? Besides accepting our obligation as world changers to confront such injustices, we have a moral reason, which is based on the belief that all people are created by God and should have the basic necessities of life. While everyone cannot live identical lives, everyone should have the opportunity to provide for their children and to improve their lives. Unfortunately, this is not the case today, as demonstrated all too clearly in Table 3.1:

TABLE 3.1

HUMAN DEVELOPMENT INDEX

The Human Development Index (HDI) is a composite index measuring average country achievement in three basic dimensions: 1) life expectancy, 2) educational attainment, and 3) adjusted real income per capita.

HDI Rank: Top 10 Countries	HDI Rank: Lowest 10 Countries
1. Norway	1. Mali
2. Sweden	2. Central African Republic
3. Canada	3. Chad
4. Belgium	4. Guinea-Bissau
5. Australia	5. Ethiopia
6. United States	6. Burkina Faso
7. Iceland	7. Mozambique
8. Netherlands	8. Burundi
9. Japan	9. Niger
10. Finland	10. Sierra Leone

Source: "Human Development Index 2002," *Human Development Report 2002,* United Nations Development Programme, 2003.

Rich nations may not think global poverty is their problem, but ultimately it is. The globalization of economic and cultural processes also means that the effects of poverty become global as well. In opening their borders for international trade, for example, countries also may be open for floods of refugees and people escaping poverty in neighboring nations. As poor countries try to become more competitive in the global marketplace, they often cut social services to their citizens, making poverty even worse. It is estimated that over one-fourth of the world's nations are so far in debt that they can never repay their loans. This great inequality between nations is a source of resentment within poor countries.

Certainly we must acknowledge that the majority of human history has been a long narrative of poverty. Most people in the past were poor, and their primary focus was simply on getting enough to eat. The last century is the only one in history to see a growing number of people have a secure food supply. While many still suffer from poverty, a minority in developed nations have been able to gain enough food for subsistence, and are focused on other forms of consumption, including material goods, entertainment, and travel. While it used to be that most people everywhere were mainly concerned with survival, now the gap between poor and rich countries is widening. With that reality has come the question: Why are so many people poor, while others have their basic needs met?

The Scope of the Problem

Although great economic growth occurred in the late nineteenth and twentieth centuries, most of this was limited to certain countries. Wealth was (and is) unevenly distributed around the world. Some analysts predicted that this gap would close in the latter part of the twentieth century but, in fact, poor countries became poorer. This was due in part to the burden borne by poorer countries to repay the debt on loans they took out during the 1960s and 1970s. By the 1980s, conditions in these countries worsened as prices fell for their commodities, internal political instability and border conflicts diverted resources, and populations dramatically increased.

An Incredible Imbalance

It is estimated that of the world's six billion people, one billion live in total poverty, with no health services, no economic resources, and not enough to eat. Another two billion survive at subsistence level, without adequate sanitation or access to clean water. An additional two billion maintain a fragile existence at the bottom of the world's economy, with no job security, property, or savings.

This girl in Latin America is starting to work at a young age, like many children in the Two-Thirds World.

Of the remaining one billion people, only about half really have any kind of stability or comfort in their lives, including regular work and meals. Yet, this small number controls about 85 percent of global wealth and uses up a majority of the world's resources. The world's 350 billionaires (in U.S. dollars) have a net worth that is estimated to be greater than that held by 45 percent of the earth's population, an incredible imbalance of economic wealth.[2]

Poverty and Disease

Compounding these problems are health issues. In many poor nations, infectious diseases such as respiratory infections, malaria, and even measles kill millions of people every year. Over two million children die annually from diarrheal diseases alone. All these are preventable, but poverty and pollution create conditions that make prevention and treatment extremely difficult, if not impossible. Tuberculosis has infected almost a third of the world's population, killing three million a year.[3] Malaria remains a major problem, spread over one hundred countries and killing about one million people a year.

HIV/AIDS deaths have also increased to over three million a year, with the large majority of these deaths occurring in poor countries. The social impact of losing so many people—most in their prime productive years—is now becoming evident. Developing nations are losing skilled workers, children are being orphaned, and the United Nations estimates that annual economic growth in many African countries is falling by .5 to 1.2 percent each year because of the impact of HIV/AIDS.[4]

No One Is Immune

Even in the world's wealthiest nations and despite economic growth, many people live in poverty. In the United States the overall *percentage* of those in poverty has dropped over the last fifty years (to almost 12 percent), but the *numbers* have increased (to thirty-three million, due to population growth). There is homelessness even in the midst of prosperity, and more children, in particular, are living below the poverty line. Bankruptcies and the ratio of debt to personal income have risen sharply in the same period. Many who are reasonably well off are carrying an enormous amount of debt, including credit cards, mortgages, and student loans. And even with health care insurance (and an estimated 40 percent of Americans don't have that coverage), most families could be financially ruined by a major illness. Thus, poverty is not just a problem of the less developed countries, although the problem in the Two-Thirds World is certainly more severe.

Globalization: More Benefits or More Problems?

On one hand, globalization has allowed free trade, the movement of capital, and the production of material goods all around the world. This in turn has led to global competition, encouraging some businesses to sacrifice workers' well-being for corporate profits. Of course, this kind of greed is nothing new, but what *is* new is the scale and number of people who are affected.

On the other hand, there are those who feel that the benefits of the global economy outweigh the problems. They point out that more people have been brought out of poverty in the last fifty years than in the previous five hundred years. Relatively speaking, this is true. Even the critics of globalization acknowledge that many people are better off because they now have jobs. At the same time, they say, we can't ignore the widening gap between the world's rich and the much larger number of poor. As the poor become more aware of these differences and have less hope of escaping their poverty, they may develop more anger toward the rich and be more receptive to extreme "solutions," whether political, economic, or religious. They also may be willing to engage in criminal acts like drug dealing or terrorism, which are both growing international threats.

Seeking Solutions

Regarding the problem of global poverty, many solutions are under discussion. Those who support a market approach believe that poor nations can improve their circumstances by private enterprise, open markets, unrestricted trade, and a legal system that allows reliable commercial relations. They believe the market approach will promote economic growth that will spread benefits to more people. They reject the idea that economies should be state controlled, pointing out that just that sort of central planning resulted in the failure of communist systems in the twentieth century. Thus, they maintain that central planning should not be duplicated in poor nations today.

A growing number of young people will need work in order to move out of poverty.

Others feel that individual initiative is not enough by itself, but also should include a partnership between governments and businesses. Working together, they can better solve the complex causes of poverty in cooperation with local groups at the community grassroots level. They believe that relying only on the market and individual self-interest will not provide a solid foundation for a "civil society" in which people are able to adequately meet their needs.

Almost everyone agrees that it is vital in the next decades to create employment opportunities for the growing number of young people who will want to join the workforce in nonagricultural jobs. As incomes rise, people then invest more in their futures, and have resources for health care and education. With better health and education generally comes a lower birthrate. This contributes to the stability needed for further economic and social progress, giving greater hope to the next generation.

GLOBAL ENVIRONMENT

In the last century, humanity has done a great deal of damage to the global environment, contributing to poverty by threatening people's food sources and endangering their health. This damage is especially dangerous for people in poor countries, as their livelihood most often is tied to farming or other occupations closely connected to the environment.

Environmental Destruction and Its Impact

Although generally the poor are more directly impacted by environmental destruction, all people worldwide are affected by one of the major effects of environmental destruction—pollution. Pollution problems include toxic waste, acid rain (air pollutants brought to earth by rain), smog, and the overuse of chemical pesticides and fertilizers. Most forms of pollution have increased significantly over the last forty years. The primary source is industrial production in wealthy nations. However, since many companies now locate factories and other industrial production facilities in poorer nations, the environmental impact today is truly global. Poor countries usually welcome economic growth, even at the cost to their environments, which potentially has serious ramifications for the future.

The growth of the world's population has put an increasing strain on the world's resources, especially food. The resulting overuse of farmlands has caused soil erosion and depletion of the earth's nutrients. For example, it is estimated that

The overcutting of forests has resulted in several global environmental problems.

over one billion metric tons of good topsoil are washed away every year.[5] Over the past fifty years, the world has lost half of its original forest cover. Deforestation, the overcutting of forests, also has resulted in major erosion. Without forests to contain runoff from rain, there is increasing and inevitable damage from floods and mudslides.

Global warming is another concern. This theory states that the rise in carbon dioxide levels due to the combustion of coal, oil, and natural gas will be responsible for a rise in global temperatures. Although this is a controversial and complex issue, many scientists fear that the increase in CO_2 emissions over the last fifty years will have many more negative effects in the years ahead. These include damage to ecosystems, a reduction in crop yields, climate changes leading to drought, decreased water availability, and possible flooding as sea levels rise.

GLOBAL WARMING
The rise in global temperatures attributed to the rise of atmospheric carbon dioxide levels.

The increasing demand for energy has also created problems, especially in the use of nuclear energy. Accidents at nuclear plants, involving the release of radioactive materials, have resulted in significant damage to the environment—and to human beings, as well. Over thirty countries have nuclear power stations, including the former Soviet Union. One of the most devastating accidents took place in 1986 in Chernobyl, Ukraine, where one eyewitness detailed the confusion and panic caused by the catastrophe.[6] The Soviet government at first denied the severity of the radiation fallout, allowing a May Day parade to proceed as scheduled in the nearby capital of Kiev—a parade in which many children participated. Eventually, over 116,000 people were evacuated from the area. Radiation fallout from the accident spread over the entire Northern Hemisphere, resulting in cases of thyroid cancer in humans and birth defects in British farm animals. The contamination of the earth and its food supply from such accidents is a major concern. The long-term effects, environmentally and socially, are yet to be seen.

Limited Resources

The provision of needed resources for the earth's growing population is also a vital concern. It has been estimated that human demand for resources over the last twenty years has depleted the available supplies, overshooting by 20 percent the earth's ability to replenish these materials.[7] The traditional ways of gathering food were "friendlier" to the environment, but didn't supply enough resources. Thus, new methods were developed, many of which put the achievement of short-term goals before long-term negative effects. One example in the fishing industry is the modern trawl method. The use of technology and larger nets led to larger yields, so much so that the North Atlantic cod population virtually has been depleted. This has effectively wiped out the local fishing industry as well. To allow the cod population to recover, Canada has banned cod fishing in its waters—although this may not be enough to reverse the damage. There are similar concerns for the future of salmon in the North Pacific.

A critical environmental issue today is the lack of potable water (suitable for drinking) globally. This concern rarely crosses the minds of most Americans, who expect the water from their taps to be safe. But for much of the world (and soon even the United States) safe drinking water is a major problem. The most obvious reason is that unsafe drinking water leads to many (preventable) diseases. More than a billion people lack potable water, and three billion lack basic sanitation. In addition to scarce drinking water, many nations do not have suitable water supplies to encourage development. In 1997 the United Nations estimated that over a third of the world's population lives in nations that cannot meet their water needs (including agricultural use). This is expected to increase to one half or even *two-thirds* of the world's population by 2025, a very dangerous situation.

An adequate supply of safe water will be a major challenge in this century.

As countries face critical water shortages, the possibility of conflicts over water supplies will increase dramatically. Few options exist for settling such disputes when both sides feel a particular water supply is *their* resource alone. This frequently occurs along major rivers that border several countries. If an upstream nation overuses the water supply (e.g., building a dam), the effect on downstream nations can be devastating. Poor countries can't afford to import food, so they depend on filling that need with what they can grow themselves. Without water, this option is impossible. All of these difficulties are further aggravated by the tremendous growth in the world's population—especially in the poor nations.

Another View of the Statistics

We should note that not all opinions on environmental issues share the same gloomy forecast. Danish statistician Bjorn Lomborg holds a much more optimistic perspective.[8] Carefully analyzing figures on environmental problems, he concludes that the data in many cases are flawed and that the problems can be managed. His major argument is that many of the negative statements about environmental issues are based on short-term or isolated studies that cannot be applied to the entire world. Lomborg believes that although we certainly should be concerned about the environment, we must base our concern on solid information. We also should put our efforts where they will do the most good. He maintains that the progress we are making in most areas should not be overshadowed by the bad news that gets more attention, especially in the world's media. Although there are many who lack the basic necessities of life, Lomborg (and others) think that we can and will overcome these problems.

GLOBAL POPULATION

One issue that complicates any solutions to the world's needs is the tremendous growth of population. At the time of Christ, it is estimated that there were approximately 250 million people in the world. At the beginning of the twentieth century, the world population had grown to just under two billion people. However, by the end of the twentieth century, the world's population was over six billion, and rapidly growing. Over 80 million people are added to the world's numbers each year. The United Nations estimates that the earth's population could grow to between seven and a half and ten billion by 2050 (with a figure of around nine billion most likely), and reach twelve billion by the twenty-third century.

Population Growth in Undeveloped Nations

The reasons for this increase are complicated. Exponential growth is certainly one factor, but it doesn't explain how rapidly the earth's population has doubled again and again. Other factors are also responsible for accelerated growth rates, such as an increase in life expectancy, better nutrition, widespread vaccinations, and a reduction in death rates (especially among infants). In many parts of the world, families believe "the more children the better," both as a means of economic security and to provide more workers to support the extended family. By **extended family** we mean that in addition to the nuclear family (mother, father, and children), a household includes other close relatives—such as grandparents and great-grandparents. Thus, birth rates

EXTENDED FAMILY
A family group that is larger than the nuclear family (mother, father, children) and that includes other close relatives.

TABLE 3.2

COUNTRIES WITH LOWEST POPULATION GROWTH
1975–2000

Hungary	-.2%	Germany	.2%
Romania	-.2%	Denmark	.2%
Estonia	-.1%	Belgium	.2%
Guyana	.1%	United Kingdom	.2%
Italy	.1%	Russian Federation	.3%

COUNTRIES WITH HIGHEST POPULATION GROWTH
1975–2000

Djibouti	4.4%	Niger	3.2%
Oman	4.2%	Tanzania	3.1%
Saudi Arabia	4.1%	Syria	3.1%
Yemen	3.9%	Malawi	3.1%
Ivory Coast	3.5%	Angola	3.0%

COUNTRIES WITH LOWEST PROJECTED POPULATION GROWTH
2000–2015

Russian Federation	-.6%	Czech Republic	-.2%
Latvia	-.6%	Switzerland	-.2%
Hungary	-.5%	Spain	-.2%
Romania	-.3%	Sweden	-.2%
Italy	-.3%	Austria	-.2%

COUNTRIES WITH HIGHEST PROJECTED POPULATION GROWTH
2000–2015

Niger	3.6%	Oman	3.2%
Uganda	3.4%	Burkina Faso	3.2%
Dem. Rep. of Congo	3.3%	Angola	3.1%
Sierra Leone	3.2%	Saudi Arabia	3.0%
Solomon Islands	3.2%	Chad	3.0%

Source: *Human Development Report 2002*, United Nations Development Programme, 2003.

continue to be high in poor countries that don't have government programs for the elderly. Large families and the "division of labor" they imply worked well in agriculture-based societies, even in the United States during the colonial and frontier eras. However, this concept doesn't work as well in an urban context.

Internal and External Migration

This population pressure has led to strains on the world's food supply and standard of living. Over half of the earth's people now live in urban areas. This number is increasing every year, primarily because of the migration of young people who hope to escape extreme poverty and find a better future. Overcrowding has led to huge slums; in fact, the United Nations estimates that half of the urban population in LDCs lives in slums. Large cities in these nations cannot provide even minimal standards of housing, infrastructure, health, education, and social services. This growth is usually due to high birth rates in LDCs, based on local traditions and the "hoped for" economic security of large families. Eighty percent of the world's population lives in developing countries, which are the world's poor nations. Ninety-eight percent of the world's population growth also occurs in these countries. The local governments often are overwhelmed by this growth and cannot provide basic necessities.

Economic Imbalance

Unfortunately, this means that the largest population growth is occurring in countries that generally have the lowest economic growth. Thus, future job seekers may not be able to find employment, furthering the nations' economic problems. Even when the annual growth rate is small, big countries still add large numbers to their populations. For example, although India's growth rate is under 2 percent per year, it still adds fifteen million new people annually. China's growth rate is under 1 percent, but it stills adds over ten million people each year.

Large populations increase the workforce but, ironically, when these people live in poverty, the availability of food, housing, and other services is inadequate. Family resources are divided into smaller pieces for family members, meaning their needs are not adequately met. This leads to internal and external migrations of people looking for work and a more promising future. A current estimate is that over 100 million people cross borders every year looking for work. Often these people have unstable lives, are not a part of any real community, and have no health coverage or education. This in turn can create deep resentment in local groups, resulting in violence or discrimination and openness to radical and extremist viewpoints.

> Unfortunately, the largest population growth is occurring in countries that generally have the lowest economic growth.

Population Growth in Developed Nations

Most industrial nations have the opposite problem. Their birth rates don't allow for the replacement of their populations, at the same time that their life expectancy rates have risen. Japan and many European countries have such low birth rates that their populations may fall by one-fourth over the next forty years. If this occurs, nations such as Japan won't have enough workers to support their aging populations. More elderly people will need support from a reduced number of workers. The worst case is Italy (with a fertility rate of 1.17 children per woman), where the population will fall by half over the next century, from over 66 million to less than 36 million. Some call this trend "collective suicide." While this may be an extreme statement, it accurately summarizes the future for some countries—especially those that do not want to allow immigration. These countries have a more similar or *homogeneous* population and, therefore, are not as willing to accept foreigners.

> **DEMOGRAPHIC COLLAPSE**
> When the reproductive rate is so low that the population declines.

A Demographic Collapse

This demographic collapse is a real possibility in most of Europe where the current population of 725 million may drop to 600 million by the year 2050. A **demographic collapse** occurs when the reproductive rate is so low that the

A declining birth rate and an emphasis on small family structure have led to major population declines in some countries.

population declines. European governments are trying to reverse the trend with child subsidies and tax credits, extended paid maternity leaves, free childcare, and other rewards for having children. In Japan the situation is especially serious, with the population expected to fall from 126 million to 55 million over the next century. The future of Japan as a world economic power is very much at risk if this happens.

The declining birth rate in these countries is due primarily to the rising cost of raising children and the entry of more women into the workforce. The United States has had a declining birth rate for the last thirty years, with not enough births to replace those who have died. Even though it is estimated that the proportion of people over sixty-five will increase from 12 percent to 20 percent of the American population, the United States will continue to add people to its population. This growth in America is due to immigration, with over 800,000 legal immigrants entering the country each year.[9]

GLOBAL POLITICS

During the last half of the twentieth century, most people assumed that the world was made up of many nations or nation-states and that these nation-states as a politically organized frame of reference would remain stable. A **nation** or nation-state is a group of people composed of one or more nationalities and possessing a defined territory and form of government. We think of nations (or countries) as a way of grouping people by territory and/or government. This is the only politically structured system that we are familiar with, and naturally most of us believe it is the "normal" way to organize and govern an area or a group.

> **NATION**
> A group of people composed of one or more nationalities and possessing a defined territory and form of government.

The Birth of Nations

But nation-states as we know them today have only existed since the eighteenth century. Most countries were founded in the nineteenth and twentieth centuries. In 1800 the world had twenty-three formal nations; by 1940 there were still only sixty-nine. In the next sixty years, over one hundred twenty-five more countries were established. However, there is a real question

CHART 3.1

FREE, PARTLY FREE, AND NON-FREE NATIONS

"Free" means having civil liberties and freedom of expression, rule of law and human rights, ability to vote and multi-party elections, freedom of association, personal autonomy, and economic rights, including private property, etc.

With this definition, the number of nations is grouped as follows:

"Free"	=	85
"Partly Free"	=	59
"Not Free"	=	48

Source: Freedom House Inc., Washington, D.C., 2000. Accessed at http://www.freedomhouse.org/ratings.

about the legitimacy of many of these governments. As the main legal institution that claims authority within its borders, governments have a monopoly on power, regardless of whether or not it reflects the will of its population. In fact, it is estimated that only 28 percent of nations are "free"— with civil liberties and political rights, including the right to choose their leaders. The remaining nations have various levels of freedom, from "partially free" to "not free" at all.

In recent years, the importance of the nation-state has diminished as economic power has shifted to corporations. Many governments are poor and depend on foreign investment or foreign aid in order to have resources to serve their populations. This reduces their credibility as governing bodies in the eyes of their citizens. In addition, more businesses are now global. Information is flowing across borders and most truly important economic decisions are not made by governments, but by multinational companies. The flow of information is especially important—previously governments controlled this flow for their own advantage. Now, due to the Internet and other media sources, controlling the flow of information is impossible. People can access information and make decisions themselves about what is true and whether they should believe their leaders. Many nations increasingly have become involved in a system of mutual dependency, where their power is really shared with business interests.

The Ethnic Dimension

Most countries are in reality a mixture of different regions that vary widely in their "economies" (including standards of living) and their cultures. In nations with several competing ethnic groups, there can be a decline or even

Ethnic divisions in the former Soviet Union contributed to its collapse.

disappearance of the central government's authority. The state structure—often put into place by colonial authorities before they left—can be inadequate to govern effectively and meet the needs of the population. In some cases it loses all control, and the people turn to traditional associations like clans or ethnic groups for the support they need. Competing groups in a country (often the case) can cause conflicts that the central government is powerless to stop.

A good example of this is the former Yugoslavia. This multiethnic state fell apart in stages in the 1990s because the citizens' loyalty to their groups was greater than their loyalty to the nation. One of the most significant events of this kind, of course, was the collapse of the Soviet Union, when one of the world's largest nations split apart after the failure of communism. We should note that only half of the citizens of the Soviet Union were "Russians," a particular ethnic group. The rest were made up of various Slavic and Muslim groups. This mixture of ethnic peoples in the former Soviet Union continues to be problematic today.

In other cases, the issue is whether people want to be citizens of their country at all. With the exception of the United States, most nations have internal separatist movements that want to break away and become independent. These groups, often ethnic or religious minorities, work seriously to create their own countries. The differentiation can even be linguistic, as with the French minority in Quebec, Canada. Many of these groups, such as the Kurds in Turkey and Iraq, essentially are not represented by their "national" governments. It is estimated that there are over 5,000 ethnic groups in the world; no one really knows how many may want to establish their own homeland nations.

Of course, the United States did experience the Civil War in the mid-nineteenth century. Some say that historical distance has caused Americans to diminish the impact of the Civil War, relegating it to the forgotten past. Others say that this precarious time in American history taught a lesson so valuable that it has been embedded in the collective consciousness of the nation—one way of explaining why the United States remains intact so many years later, with no serious internal threats to its unity.

The Future of the Nation-State

A key challenge in the realm of global politics is how to ensure that people are truly represented by their governments. Even in the twenty-first century, too many "premodern" governments still exist by force and repression, reminiscent of the chaotic situation in medieval Europe. In addition, some modern states that seem to have democratic structures in place are in fact ruled by a powerful elite. In both these situations, citizens are not truly free and cannot achieve their true potential. Those seeking equity in global politics hope that by being exposed to other societies, these repressed nations will demand more freedom and other positive changes within their countries.

Because of globalization, some think the nation-state as we know it will eventually disappear, but this is unlikely. The majority of the world's citizens are loyal to their countries and committed to keeping them intact as nation-states. Even separatist groups usually want to establish a nation for themselves. Others fear that governments will just become puppets of multinational corporations. This is indeed a more viable possibility, especially for many small countries. In general, the most realistic scenario may be that nations will continue to exist, but will increasingly allow more cross-cultural and cross-border contact and trade, enabling their citizens to have independence and autonomy in all parts of their lives.

Nations as they are organized today may change dramatically in the next century.

GLOBAL CONFLICT AND SECURITY

International Disputes

Because of the problems we have described, it is clear that issues of international conflicts and security will continue to be significant concerns in the twenty-first century. Potential problems include disputes over natural resources (such as water in the Middle East or diamonds in Africa). These resources are limited, making them extremely valuable for poor nations. Nations are even willing to go to war to retain or gain control of these resources.

Other internal conflicts and threats to international security include unemployment and illegal immigration. Although we have looked at these problems as by-products of global poverty, it is easy to see how they are related to the issue of global conflict and security. Unemployment in poor nations is especially rampant among the young, which can lead to social unrest and crime. It also results in illegal immigration as people search for work, resulting in huge costs for the countries "hosting" these illegal immigrants. They bring in foreign cultures and languages that often conflict with the resentful indigenous society.

When a nation's government is unable to control its borders or maintain order, its own security and that of neighboring countries can be compromised.

More seriously, separatist movements or groups within countries (such as the Basque separatist party in Europe) often feel justified in using force to achieve their objectives. Generally, these groups are extremely committed to their causes and will not accept compromises. Border disputes (such as in many parts of Latin America) are also particularly volatile because these areas contain historical and emotional symbolism regarding the "homeland." Citizens of these nations believe the territory rightfully belongs to them, regardless of opposition.

The actual breakup of countries (such as Yugoslavia, during which over 200,000 were killed) is especially dangerous; violent tensions usually are not resolved by the split and in fact can worsen. We have seen many ethnic or tribal conflicts escalate into such atrocities as those of Rwanda in 1994, resulting in genocide and mass migrations of people seeking to escape execution at the hands of the "victors." Regional conflicts in countries like China potentially could erupt into civil war. In these situations, the conflict often spills over to neighboring nations, drawing them into the dispute or creating huge numbers of refugees. In either event, the international community has not yet developed effective ways to intervene and stop these disputes, the results of which can threaten international security.

International Crime

In addition, global security faces the growing threat of international crime, which flourishes across open borders. Russia is one such country in which criminal groups are virtually free to do what they want, as the government is powerless to stop them. In nations like Columbia, criminal elements use violence to intimidate both the government authorities and the local population. Even military intervention is usually ineffective in such situations. Of particular concern today are terrorist groups, which use a variety of destructive tactics to intimidate and spread fear. As we learned on September 11, 2001, large-scale terrorist attacks can have major social and economic repercussions—a multiplying impact, as companies go out of business and people stop traveling, for example. With greater access to dangerous technologies, and the lack of security at many nuclear and biochemical facilities, the threat of future terrorist attacks is very real.

Religion and Global Conflict

Because religion is central to so many cultures, it also is a potential source of conflict. As Western culture has become more "secular," some feel it will inevitably clash with other societies that have strong religious beliefs. This may be especially true of Islamic societies, which have used the Muslim religion to reshape their societies, as well as to justify political acts.[10] In some cases these Islamic movements are motivated by a belief that Islamic societies have been persecuted by colonial or Western nations. In other cases they are motivated by a belief that Islam has been "corrupted" in some way and must be protected by stricter controls. Many large countries, including Nigeria, Indonesia, and the Philippines, will experience increasing tensions between Muslims and Christians, which could potentially lead to religious wars.

> **RELIGIOUS TOTALITARIANISM**
> The situation that occurs when a particular religious group imposes its ideology on others, usually by force.

Although there are many different religious sects within Islam, most of the world's Muslims live in countries in which they are the majority group. Because of this, they have been able to impose their

The Islamic world is an area of potential religious conflict.

interpretation of culture, law, human rights, and spirituality on the citizens of these nations. When the central government is weak and the people are dissatisfied with their living conditions, extreme religious movements can offer simple "solutions" that may appear attractive to many residents who have no other hope. Anti-American views are often part of these movements, either because some of these individuals feel that the United States is anti-Muslim, or because America is an easy target for their hatred of the West in general (and what it represents). These movements span the globe, from Sudan to Iran, from Pakistan to some of the former Soviet republics. The essential problem here is religious intolerance, or what some call **religious totalitarianism**—a situation that occurs when a particular religious group imposes its ideology on others, usually by force. It is motivated by a belief that one religion is supreme and must rule over all others—an unacceptable position at any time, but especially wrong today.

RESPONDING TO THE CHALLENGES

In this chapter, we have very briefly covered the needs challenging the world today. The question now is what to do about all these challenges. Some questions that we should consider are:

- Should countries be responsible for their own problems, despite the reality of globalization? Or are there good reasons for others to be involved in problem solving?

- Should rich nations be held more accountable for these global problems—primarily because they benefited in the past from poorer nations' raw materials and benefit today from their cheap labor?

- Should industrial nations clean up pollution because they are the main contributors to this problem?

- What is the responsibility of wealthier nations that once had colonies and built their own economies with the resources they obtained from these colonies?

A good deal of debate continues on whether the Two-Thirds World countries would be better off today if they had never been colonized by the West. Of course, this question is impossible to answer, as history cannot be rewritten.

Certainly there was exploitation of people and resources—this has been documented. But what if colonialism had not occurred? If it had not, it is unlikely that these countries would be integrated into the global economy in any significant way. Author and political analyst Dinesh D'Souza argues that these former colonies may be *better off* than if they had not been colonized.[11] With colonialism came important infrastructures: the building of roads and railroads and the development of irrigation systems. Colonized countries were structured to include organized legal systems. The colonizing nations provided education (for some) and promoted their Western values—including the essential idea of freedom. Although the colonists didn't necessarily believe in freedom for their subjects, this idea was transmitted through their institutions and eventually worked its way into the consciousness of the people.

But the question remains: what should we do *today* to address the problems that are critical for the survival of all people, regardless of where they reside?

The Continuum of National Development

Most people in Western countries—especially Americans—view their own experience as the model upon which other countries should pattern their national development. Americans take it for granted that the American way of doing things is the best way, and naturally should be used by others. This is

The Western idea of "progress" is a model for some countries, but not others.

particularly true in economic matters. Chapter 2 briefly reviewed the idea of progress as the belief that things will continue to improve, and how it is a uniquely Western/American belief that forms a foundation for the way Americans think and act. Americans and other Westerners operate on the assumption that as people are exposed to a "modern" way of life, they will want to adopt it for themselves. They assume that as people see the benefits of "progress," they will want to have a similar lifestyle, including comparable education, work, and standard of living. To make this happen, they generally conclude, all that is needed for other nations to "catch up" to the United States is a transfer of education and technology.

The presupposition underlying this view is that all countries can be placed on a continuum of economic stages through which they must pass in order to become "developed." Of course, the Western nations are at the top of this continuum. Others can move up the continuum by giving up their traditional practices and adopting Western technology and "modern" values. However, things have not proven to be that simple (and still are not) as poorer countries have attempted to follow this model. Many people around the world choose to keep their own cultures, and are not pleased with Western (especially American) values. Among some there is a concern that American values stress too much individualism, monetary wealth, and personal freedom (at the expense of the family, the group, the culture, etc.). Still others contend that there should be a way to develop economically without having to become American culturally.

Sustainable Development

What most people *do* agree on is the need for sustainable development, which is not dependent on external subsidies or continual foreign aid. **Sustainable development** is community development that can be continued by local people, mainly with local resources. This concept goes beyond the idea of using the environment in sustainable ways (although it does include this idea, of course). Sustainable development can be achieved by the creation of a stable infrastructure, with reliable communication and transportation services, as well as a stable political environment, with a legal

SUSTAINABLE DEVELOPMENT
Community development that can be continued by local people, mainly with local resources.

framework and equitable laws. With this foundation, people also need access to credit so that small businesses can be established. If these businesses can effectively market their products, both domestically and internationally, the income can be reinvested for economic growth. This in turn creates more jobs, which leads to greater economic development, which then provides more resources for the infrastructure of a nation—and the cycle of sustainability continues.

> Conventional development assumes that the Western level of consumption is the "right" way for everyone, but is this realistic?

However, "development" means more than just economic sustainability. The United States certainly has a strong tendency to use economic indicators to measure well-being, as we saw in chapter 2 of this text. In many other regions, people are more concerned with family ties, other relationships, and a sense of community—accomplishments that aren't measurable. When they think of "sustainability," they are referring to the maintenance of their way of life and the traditions that are an essential part of their culture.

Others wonder if there are enough resources in the world for everyone to have a Western style of development. They ask not only if this is possible (and conclude it isn't), but also if it is ethical. As they see it, globalized Western development would use up the earth's resources in a way that cannot be sustained. Some feel this level of consumption is fundamentally wrong, as it puts an emphasis on things instead of people, and on growth instead of community. Conventional development assumes that the Western level of consumption is the "right" way for everyone, but is this realistic?

The World Bank, which is supported by many developed countries, lends over $50 billion a year to poor nations for their development. However, there is actually little to show for all this investment. Governments and non-governmental agencies contribute additional billions of dollars to alleviate poverty, usually with the same minimal results. Clearly, we must come up with a new approach to resolving the needs of the world, as money certainly isn't the only or even the best answer. We must develop and implement new ideas, exemplifying true partnership between rich and poor countries, and involving both governments and other groups. With this involvement, perhaps we *can* achieve a new future, based not on traditional development, or even sustainable development, but on true human development.

Beyond Development

It should be clear that we face tremendous global challenges. The key word is "face"—ignorance is not an option! Each of these areas of global need is significant for our future and we must understand them if we are to resolve them. To summarize the needs:

FIGURE 3.1

SUMMARY OF GLOBAL NEEDS

GLOBAL POVERTY
• Income Imbalance
• Increased Disease

GLOBAL ENVIRONMENT
• Pollution Problems
• Limited Resources

GLOBAL CONFLICTS/SECURITY
• International Disputes
• Religious Conflicts

GLOBAL POPULATION
• Growth/Decline
• Economic Disparities

GLOBAL POLITICS
• Ethnic Tensions
• Future of Nation-States

"It's Not My Problem"

We can respond to these almost overwhelming needs with pessimism. This attitude leads people to give up, to feel helpless in the face of so many troubles.

They may also choose to believe that global issues are not their problem; therefore, their help isn't required. Or they may choose to believe that since these problems are the fault of others, let those involved solve their own problems. This essentially means that the people *with* the problem must solve it themselves because they *caused* it.

A natural progression of this mind-set is that people with needs simply must work harder, as Americans do, and everything will work out. It assumes their economies will respond to hard work and the wise use of resources. This mind-set also can take a paranoid twist: All disadvantaged people want to move to the United States and take advantage of its standard of living, which Americans have built because they did things better and were better organized. Essentially, this viewpoint is based on fear, the fear of losing what one culture has that another culture does not have. Underlying this fear is the sense that little if anything can actually be done, so what's the point?

"Nothing New under the Sun"

A second possible response to global needs is to think that things will "just work out," that "all will be fine" eventually. This seemingly optimistic view assumes that problems have always been resolved in the past and they'll surely be resolved in the future. The problems are perhaps not all that bad, and life will go on as it has throughout history. This is essentially an isolationist perspective, avoiding involvement in others' lives. It also may include an element of superiority. For example, some maintain that just as America pulled itself out of the Great Depression, others must do the same. Like the pessimistic perspective above, this viewpoint comes

> An isolationist perspective means avoiding involvement in others' lives.

around to a "hands off" policy—let them work out their own problems without involving us. Besides, don't we have enough needs of our own? Why take on others? After all, we're already supporting global charities—isn't that enough?

"Opportunity Knocking"

A third possible response is to see global needs as opportunities. The challenges can be an inspiration to do something, no matter how small. This perspective encourages a search for new and better ideas, to solve problems in partnership with others. It strives to be creative, to move out of one's cultural assumptions (while realistically acknowledging that this is very difficult). Essentially an activist position, it implies the desire to make a difference in the

One perspective on how to meet global needs is to view them as an opportunity for partnership to improve people's lives.

world. This perspective does not gloss over the seriousness of global needs, but believes something *can* be done. It believes in connecting local people with outsiders and encouraging them to work in partnership, as each has a unique perspective on the problems and different resources to offer. Because each situation is different and requires a special approach, this perspective realizes the usefulness of studying change methods and finding the appropriate ones to use.

How Should Christians Respond?

Christians must not forget the spiritual dimension of responding to global needs. Although these problems exist in a physical world, they also raise interesting questions about the nonphysical realm. Not all Christians agree on how to resolve global needs. For example, some Christians believe that God will intervene and solve everything, either by returning to earth or by destroying it. Therefore, any action on the Christian's part to improve things is fruitless and may even work against God's perfect plan. Others believe that God is returning soon and will judge non-Christians, so the most important issue is not people's needs but rather their spiritual state. This perspective may contain the idea that Christians are God's blessed people, so it is His priority to take care of them, regardless of what happens to the rest of the world.

Still another Christian response is that it is all up to them to solve these problems. This is the position of **Christian social activism,** which maintains that Christians are essentially given the duty of helping others. Although it refers to God, this response can give the impression that Christians are basically on their own, that God expects them to use their talents and resources to help the poor. An underlying assumption is that the needs are caused by social injustice and Western exploitation.

> ## CHRISTIAN SOCIAL ACTIVISM
> The belief that Christians are given the duty to help those whose problems are caused by social injustice and Western exploitation.

Therefore, individuals from the West are particularly responsible for solving these problems. Christian social activism also assumes that human beings are God's method of bringing about change. If Christians fail, the needs will not be met. Therefore, they must do their best and hope that God will be pleased by their efforts.

A fourth Christian response blends elements of the other three: Christians should do all that they can, but they must also look to God for His direction and strength. This perspective is based on the belief that God *does* care about His creation, especially every human being that He made. He will ultimately redeem the world but, in the meantime, people must assist one another. The world's wealthy in particular will be held responsible for how they used the resources with which they were entrusted. In this view, we are all stewards of His world and are called on to help solve this world's problems, but we are not ultimately responsible for meeting all the needs. The final determination of the future is in God's hands.

KEY CONCEPTS
Christian social activism
demographic collapse
extended family
global warming
LDCs
MNCs
nation
religious totalitarianism
sustainable development

However we respond to global needs, we first must realize that these needs are constantly changing. Therefore, responses will have to be tailored to each unique situation. Like a fast-moving river, the world and its challenges are always in a state of flux. Therefore, every potential response must be carefully researched and predicated on the actual current situation. (Some tools for this kind of observation will be outlined in chapter 8.) To be effective, we must also understand the process of change, a topic to which we turn in the next four chapters.

QUESTIONS FOR DISCUSSION

1. What do you think causes global poverty? Is it everyone's fault, or the fault of particular nations?

2. Which environmental problems are especially critical today? What do you think should be done to solve or reduce these problems?

3. Of the responses to global needs covered at the end of this chapter, which are closest to your own views? Explain your reasons.

ENDNOTES

1. Gordon Brown, "FfD [Financing for Development] and Children," *Global Future* (Fall 2002): 3.
2. Susan R. Shreve and Porter Shreve, eds., *How We Want to Live: Narratives on Progress in America* (Boston: Beacon Press, 1998).
3. Thomas F. Homer-Dixon, *The Ingenuity Gap: How Will We Solve the Problems of the Future?* (New York: Knopf Publishers, 2000).
4. Worldwatch Institute, *State of the World 2002* (New York: W. W. Norton & Company, 2002).
5. Mary H. Cooper, "Population and the Environment," in *Global Issues: Selections from the CQ Researcher* (Washington, D.C.: CQ Press, 2001).
6. Interview with Anna X, September 2002, conducted by co-author John Johnson.
7. Mathis Wackernagel, et. al., "Tracking the Ecological Overshoot of the Human Economy," *Proc. Natl. Acad. Sci. USA*, 99, no. 14, (July 9, 2002): 9266-71. (www.pnas.org or for direct access to abstract http://www.pnas.org/cgi/content/abstract/142033699v1)
8. Bjorn Lomborg, *The Skeptical Environmentalist: Measuring the Real State of the World* (Cambridge: Cambridge University Press, 1998).
9. Cooper, "Population and the Environment."
10. See Samuel Huntington, *The Clash of Civilizations and the Remaking of World Order* (New York: Simon & Schuster, 1996).
11. Dinesh D'Souza, "Two Cheers for Colonialism," in *The Chronicle of Higher Education* 48, no. 35 (May 10, 2002): B7.

CHAPTER FOUR

Understanding the Process of Change

Understanding the needs of our world should call us to action. Can we be content when injustice abounds in the world? Should we be passive when faced with the world's many problems, only a few of which were covered in chapter 3? Many conscientious individuals today agree that they must act and they must act now. The more difficult issue, however, is knowing what to do. How do we respond to the world's needs and bring about change?

JOHN WOOLMAN: AN EFFECTIVE CHANGE AGENT

In the 1700s, it was common practice for professing Christians to own slaves. Some Christian slave owners even defended themselves biblically, interpreting Scriptures that recognized the existence of slavery in Bible times as a way to justify its practice centuries later.

American Quaker John Woolman stood against slavery, dedicating his entire adult life to the elimination of this practice. Over a twenty-year period, he visited wealthy Quaker farmers along the East Coast. Rather than criticize or confront them directly about slave ownership (a method they would have resisted), he simply asked them questions such as these:

- "What does it mean to be a person of integrity?"
- "What does it mean to own a slave?"
- "What does it mean to will a slave to one's children?"

Driven by his desire to bring about change, he persisted, visiting farm after farm. By 1770, nearly one hundred years before the Civil War, not a single Quaker owned a slave. Thus, the Quakers were the first religious group to denounce and renounce slavery. Robert Greenleaf points out:

> One wonders what would have been the result if there had been fifty John Woolmans or even five, traveling the length and breadth of the colonies in the eighteenth century persuading people, one by one, with gentle non-judgmental argument that a wrong should be righted by individual voluntary action. Perhaps we would not have had the war with its 600,000 casualties and the impoverishment of the South, and with the resultant vexing social problem that is at fever heat 100 years later with no end in sight. We know now, in the perspective of history, that just a slight alleviation of the tension in the 1850's might have avoided the war. A few John Woolmans, just a few, might have made the difference.[1]

John Woolman understood the needs of his world and determined to bring about change. He saw an evil system that rewarded some individuals and oppressed others. Wisely and prudently, he challenged this evil and changed the system.

Unsuccessful Change Agents

Not all change agents have been as effective as John Woolman. Critics of change are quick to point out its potential for negative impact. We cannot deny that careless change agents have done much damage throughout history. A worst-case example can be found in the actions of the Union Carbide Plant of Bhopal, India. In its effort to produce jobs for the local economy (and, of course, make a profit), Union Carbide overlooked a critical element: the maintenance of the hardware containing a toxic gas. As a result, the gas leaked, killing 2,500 people and injuring 200,000 others.[2] Additional examples of this kind include the Christian Crusades, the nuclear disaster at Chernobyl (see chapter 3), and the attempts of the United States to change Vietnam. These tragedies and others like them help us realize that good intentions alone do not make us effective. If we wish to bring about change, we must understand the process through which change occurs.

The topic of change is very popular, evidenced by the quantity and variety of resources available today. While we cannot possibly summarize all change theories, we will focus on areas that are useful to our discussion of global issues. In this chapter we will provide an overview of change. In chapter 5 we will look at ways that individuals and organizations can facilitate change. Chapters 6 and 7 offer examples of successful change agents, profiling the lives of individuals who have practiced the principles outlined in this book. Chapter 8 then briefly discusses specific methods for understanding cultures and organizations.

The Process of Change: How Does It Happen?

A few years ago, co-author John Johnson stood on the central square of Kiev, Ukraine. He watched a crowd of smartly dressed Ukrainians mill around the square with different objectives in mind. Some sought entertainment, others enjoyed the fountains, while still others waited for friends. He also noticed another visiting American standing nearby. Dressed in worn jeans and wearing a backpack, he exemplified the casual American look. However,

The central square in Kiev, Ukraine.

as Ukrainians passed him, he confronted them with what he felt was wrong in their society. Because he did not speak the local language, he had hired an interpreter to translate and communicate his point of view. After several failed attempts, he turned to his interpreter with a frown. "Sasha, they won't listen," he said. "Let's go home."

Why did he fail to get his message across? The square was clearly the place to be. Other people there drew large crowds, including salespeople, cult leaders, and proponents of strange medicines. One of the biggest attractions was a band from Peru, South America, a country even farther away from Kiev than the United States. The problem was not this American's attire (although inappropriate by local standards). It was not his inability to speak the language, something most people will forgive. This man's problem was that he did not understand the process of change. He seemed to feel that if individuals were just exposed to his ideas, they would understand and immediately practice them, an all-too-common mistake with marketers today.

So, exactly how does change occur? In this chapter, we will cover five major approaches to the process of change. These change models are categorized as:

- Evolutionary
- Individualistic
- Functional
- Symbolic
- Interactionist

We will conclude the chapter with a discussion of the five social contexts in which change occurs.

TABLE 4.1	
UNDERSTANDING THE PROCESS OF CHANGE	
FIVE APPROACHES TO CHANGE	**FIVE DIFFERENT CONTEXTS IN WHICH CHANGE OCCURS**
Evolutionary Model	Egalitarian Society
Individualistic Model	Individualistic Society
Functional Model	Hierarchical Society
Symbolic Model	Fatalistic Society
Interactionist Model	Autonomy

The Significance of Culture

Before we can discuss cultural change, we should understand what it is that we are attempting to change. What do we mean by the term culture? In chapter 1 we defined culture as a particular society or group's way of life, including the values, beliefs, and norms of behavior it passes on to future generations. Culture is a learned system that shows people how to live. It provides identity, security, and shared expectations of behavior. Defining what is normal and what is not, culture provides the rules by which people live. For the purposes of this discussion, culture is a group of people's way of life, or "everything that people have, think and do as members of their society."[3]

Culture is a learned system that is passed on to each new generation.

One of the distinctive aspects of this term is the breadth of its inclusion. For example, when we use the phrase "American culture," what do we mean? As we saw in chapter 2, a number of characteristics put together do indeed make up a distinctive way of life in the United States. However, there certainly are differences within this broad category. Are we describing the Latin Americans of Chicago, the Koreans of Los Angeles, or the white Anglo-Saxon farmers of the Midwest? Because of this term's breadth, we can use "American" to describe all of the groups mentioned above. We also can use it to discuss many different things, including a body of cultural knowledge, distinctive patterns of behavior, and a shared history. For example, all of the groups mentioned above may have a shared body of knowledge about the names George Washington and Benjamin Franklin. They may understand the meaning of the word "hamburger," although some may not know how to say it in English. On the other hand, they are not likely to be familiar with the name Taras Shevchenko (a Ukrainian hero), or the taste of *Shash-Lik*, a dish with which every Ukrainian is familiar.

The general nature of the term culture is useful, but we must be careful not to abuse it in overgeneralizations. Hardly any culture is "pure." Rather, it is a complex mixture of many perspectives and ways of life. Especially as people are exposed to other ways of life, every culture becomes a blend of beliefs and practices. For example, understanding Chinese culture means knowing that it includes a main body of knowledge and many distinctive traits that can be called "Chinese." At the same time, Chinese culture includes several individual cultural profiles, evidenced by the many subgroups that exist in this huge nation.

Understanding these basics of culture, we now can explore the question of cultural change.

TABLE 4.2				
THE FIVE APPROACHES TO CHANGE				
AN EVOLUTIONARY APPROACH	**AN INDIVIDUALISTIC APPROACH**	**A FUNCTIONAL APPROACH**	**A SYMBOLIC APPROACH**	**AN INTERACTIONIST APPROACH**
All cultures pass through a series of developments, leading in the end to developed societies.	Cultures change through the interaction of the individual and the group.	Change occurs when outside influences disturb the cultural system.	Cultural change occurs when the important symbols in a culture are put away and replaced with new ones.	Cultures change through social interaction between groups and individuals, including the exchange of ideas, gifts, and money.

Gradual Change: An Evolutionary Approach

Early social scientists in the nineteenth century and into the twentieth century viewed change from a Darwinian perspective. Based on Charles Darwin's theory of evolution, they believed that as the result of natural processes all cultures passed through a series of developments, leading in the end to fully "developed societies." Of course, these social scientists saw their own European nations as fully developed societies, considering themselves as superior in every way. As such, they were the early proponents of the idea of progress. A number of influential intellectuals adhered to this approach, among them Max Weber, Emile Durkheim, and even Sigmund Freud.

Lewis Henry Morgan's *Ancient Society* gives us an insight into this form of evolutionary thinking.[4] He believed that societies pass through three stages of development, which he called savagery, barbarianism, and civilization. Morgan thought that all cultures progressed from lower savagery to upper savagery, from upper savagery to lower barbarianism, from lower barbarianism to upper barbarianism, and finally on to civilization. It should come as no surprise that the home countries of these theorists—in Western Europe and the United States—represented "civilization." Because of their "primitive," non-European ways, tribal societies occupied the lower end of the spectrum.

> **EVOLUTIONARY CHANGE MODEL**
> A change model predicated on unilinear development; that is, societies develop in a series of stages, usually from primitive to advanced.

The logical conclusions from this **evolutionary change model** are that cultural development is unilinear and that the best adapted societies will survive and prosper. Those who are less developed are not as well equipped to meet challenges and, therefore, must be helped. In this view, change results when individuals and societies adopt features that better adapt to a changing environment. Thus, change is considered positive when it results in a more "advanced" society.

This change perspective is demonstrated by the Marxist philosophy that guided the Soviet Union and other countries for much of the twentieth century. According to Karl Marx, change would inevitably come about as capitalistic societies faced the contradictions and problems of their socio-economic systems and eventually evolved into a communist state. This implied that the process would produce successive structural reorganizations throughout all sectors of society. Of course, this philosophy wasn't supported by historical events—as the collapse of communist systems in the 1990s clearly demonstrated. The Marxian approach to evolutionary change was not alone in failing; many other applications of the evolutionary approach have failed to be validated by actual events.

Looking Within: An Individualistic Approach

American Franz Boas did not agree with the evolutionary point of view. Unlike many others in the last half of the nineteenth century, he learned about

Learning another culture is best accomplished through face-to-face contact.

cross-cultural issues by becoming part of another culture, spending many years with the Kwakiutl Native Americans of the Northwest. He learned their language and was able to articulate their beliefs and practices.

Boas believed that anthropologists who supported an evolutionary approach to change lacked information upon which to base their conclusions. Rather than focusing on the complexity of the cultures they studied, they wrote in their armchairs, basing their beliefs on the writings of others. Some of their information came from untrained tourists, individuals quick to label what they did not understand as primitive or inferior. Boas believed in actual observation of cultures. His method of investigation came to be called **fieldwork** because his firsthand observation and collection of information occurred "in the field."

FIELDWORK
A method of investigation based upon firsthand observation and collection of information in the field.

Boas concluded that if people are to understand the ramifications of cultural change, anthropologists must try to explain the relationship of individual action to group custom and tradition. He also believed that the degree to which each culture is developed must be evaluated by what is important to the members of *that culture*, not by standards produced in the United States or Europe. Ruth Benedict and Margaret Mead, who had been students of Boas, built on his approach to emphasize the individuality and unique value of each culture. In the **individualistic change model,** each context is different. The people in the culture must decide the degree to which change will occur—based on their standards, not an outside standard.

> ## INDIVIDUALISTIC CHANGE MODEL
> A change model based on the relationship of individual action to group custom and tradition.

The adaptive features of some so-called "primitive" societies can serve to demonstrate this principle. For example, the Inupiaq (Eskimo) people have an incredibly detailed understanding of their environment, gained over several thousand years, which allows them to survive in the severe Arctic climate.[5] Based on a detailed study of animal behavior, their hunters have as much knowledge as another society's highly trained scientists do. Changing Inupiaq hunting methods to "modern" techniques would probably be less effective and could disturb other carefully constructed aspects of the Inupiaq culture. Change in this case should only come from within the society.

Let's Keep the Village: A Functional Approach

In England, anthropologists developed an approach of their own. One of the best known proponents of a functional change model was Bronislaw Malinowski. Originally from Poland, Malinowski studied anthropology in London, then went to the Western Pacific to complete his fieldwork requirements. World War I prevented him from returning home. As a result, his plan for a one-year stay stretched to three. He became fluent in the local language and immersed himself in the culture, describing the society in great detail.

As he reflected on his fieldwork, Malinowski came to believe that the purpose of a society is to meet the culturally defined needs of its members. To meet these needs, societies develop institutions (i.e., reoccurring patterns of activity) such as religion, art, a system of relating to others (a kinship system), and family life. With

Anthropologists often view societies as complete systems that are developed to meet the needs of their members.

its focus on the functions of each part of a society, this approach became known as functionalism. The **functional change model** is based on the functions of each part of a society. While Malinowski focused on institutions and individual behaviors, other anthropologists—such as A. R. Radcliffe-Brown—focused on the function of societal norms or rules of behavior. Radcliffe-Brown believed that nearly all relationships in a society (adult-child, man-woman, rich-poor) are regulated by such norms. Their purpose is to steer individuals through relational uncertainty and help them know how to act in a given situation. Radcliffe-Brown also stressed the role of reciprocity in uniting members of a society.

FUNCTIONAL CHANGE MODEL
A change model based on the functions of each part of a society.

Functional anthropologists believe that cultural change can be destructive to a society. In general, they believe that groups should be allowed to keep their own cultures, as these cultures serve an important function for their members. If outside elements or individuals are introduced, the careful balance between a society's institutions and its needs can be lost. Outsiders are often prone to disregard local norms (which they may not know) and throw local institutions into imbalance. Because of this, functional anthropologists generally view most change in a negative light.[6]

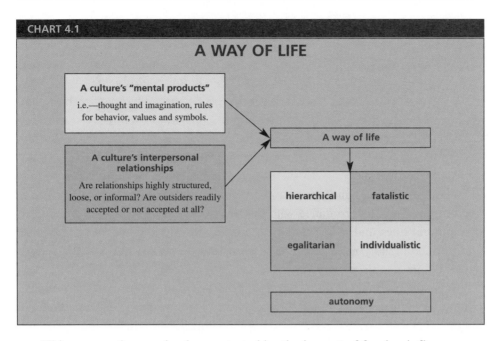

CHART 4.1

A WAY OF LIFE

A culture's "mental products"

i.e.—thought and imagination, rules for behavior, values and symbols.

A culture's interpersonal relationships

Are relationships highly structured, loose, or informal? Are outsiders readily accepted or not accepted at all?

A way of life

| hierarchical | fatalistic |
| egalitarian | individualistic |

autonomy

This perspective can be demonstrated by the impact of foreign influences on the Western Pacific nation of Papua New Guinea, which had only minimal contact with the outside world before World War II. In recent decades, increased contact has brought in better medical care and education. However, the exposure to foreign wealth has also created a desire for (and even an expectation of) prosperity that is not attainable. With few schools and even fewer jobs, the youth of PNG are constantly frustrated in their search to be more "Western." This has caused a major breakdown of traditional social customs, as young people reject their culture and even turn to crime to fulfill their new expectations. The functional model would see this as the direct result of changes upsetting the cultural balance that had sustained this society throughout its history.[7]

Culture and Meaning: A Symbolic Approach

In anthropology, interest in symbolic approaches to culture grew after World War II.[8] Anthropologists such as Mary Douglas and Victor Turner began to look below the surface of specific behaviors practiced by a people group (such as their purification rituals) to study the symbolic meanings represented in these acts.[9] Taking a similar approach, authors Michael Thompson, Richard Ellis, and Aaron Wildavsky view culture as people's "mental products," or the products of human thought and imagination.[10] Among other "products" are cultural rules for

SYMBOLIC CHANGE MODEL
A change model based on a culture's reaction to new symbols and rules of behavior.

behavior (or norms), cultural values, and cultural symbols. In other words, culture is created in people's minds. Over time, different societies decide what members should value, what they should believe about themselves and others, and what their important symbols will be.

These beliefs include how they as a society came into being, what cultural rituals are important to them, and what rules of behavior they follow. Does one bow, shake hands, or kiss in greeting? What does it mean to be on time and/or to be late? In accordance with this approach, George Spindler maintained that cultural rules and beliefs are passed on by leading members of the culture and instilled in the younger members. He believed that this not only happens at home, but in schools as well.[11]

From the perspective of the **symbolic change model,** change occurs when a culture introduces new symbols and embraces new rules of behavior. An historical example of this can be seen in the United States during the 1960s and 1970s, when new symbols of the "counterculture" were introduced to American society. These symbols led to new ideas about behavior, especially among younger people. Members of the established culture resisted these new ways. The result was conflict. In some cases conflict became quite intense, dividing families, communities, and even the nation. A worst-case example can be seen in the student protests against the Vietnam War, particularly at Kent State University in Ohio. There, the tension between the old and the new erupted into violence, with the National Guard shooting and killing four.

Culture As Relationship: An Interactionist Approach

In 1925, French anthropologist Marcel Mauss published an essay entitled "The Gift." In it he argued that gift exchange was the process by which social relationships were created and maintained in some societies. He felt that gift exchange was not just an economic transaction, but a moral transaction as well. Because acceptance of a gift often obligates the recipient to reciprocate, the relationship endures beyond the moment when the actual transaction takes place.[12]

INTERACTIONIST CHANGE MODEL
A change model based on how a culture changes because of its interaction with the outside world.

The authors of *Cultural Theory* take a similar approach, proposing that culture consists of interpersonal relationships. Proponents of this approach ask questions such as these:

- How do individuals relate to one another within a given social group?
- Are those relationships formal, structured, loose, or informal?
- Does the culture emphasize the distinction between insiders and outsiders, or does it readily accept all?

It is clear that social contexts differ in this regard. For example, the United States as a culture prizes equality, generally de-emphasizing class levels. Other societies, however, feel free to emphasize these distinctions, openly awarding privilege to those in the higher classes.[13]

According to the **interactionist change model,** change occurs in such societies when they begin to interact more with the outside world and lose their fear of it. An example of this can be seen in numerous immigrant communities within the United States. When immigrants first arrive, they continue to stress the purity of their language and culture. They place an emphasis on retaining

The interactionist change model focuses on the relationships that bring about change.

their language and distinct traditions by limiting interactions with the larger society around them. As time passes, individuals within the group attend public schools and become integrated into American society. The distinction between insider and outsider becomes less significant and sometimes disappears entirely. This occurred in co-author Boyd Johnson's family. By the second generation, his German relatives had given up their "old" language and exchanged it for English.

Sometimes, societal class levels are reduced when individuals within a society change cultural environments. Even in India's well-entrenched caste system, an individual's level in society may become blurred when that person moves to a large city and begins to interact with other professionals in a different environment. Status thus can become more dependent on credentials and profession than on one's traditional "place" in society.

CHART 4.2

FIVE WAYS OF LIFE

hierarchical	**fatalistic**
Highly structured levels. Entrance and exit procedures are either simple or do not exist at all.	Highly structured but with complete entrance and exit procedures. Not easy to enter and not easy to leave.
egalitarian	**individualistic**
Group-oriented governments. Leaders are indistinguishable from others in the group.	Freedom of choice is emphasized. Individuals can enter and leave the society at will.

autonomy

Very little interaction with others.
Withdrawal from all types of society.

Source: based on Michael Thompson, Richard Ellis, and Aaron Wildavsky, *Cultural Theory* (Boulder, CO: Westview Press, 1990).

FIVE SOCIAL CONTEXTS

To understand the implications of change, we must not only understand how individuals and groups change, but also how the society around them allows them to change and *expects* them to change. Thompson, Ellis, and Wildavsky coin the phrase "a way of life" to define their approach to culture. (See Chart 4.1.) This is the combination of a culture's mental products (symbols, norms, and values) and its pattern of social relationships. The authors hold that there are only five possible combinations of these two factors, making for five different types of social contexts:

- Egalitarian
- Individualistic
- Hierarchical
- Fatalistic
- Autonomous

Although each culture chooses one of these five as a dominant pattern, the other four patterns also may be present. For example, modern Chinese society leans towards a fatalistic social environment (described below), but the other types of social contexts are there as well (including individualism, which is a significant departure from the pattern of mainstream Chinese culture). In fact, organizations in present-day Chinese culture represent all five ways, including Buddhist monks living in solitude (autonomy), hierarchical business organizations, and communist party collectives with an egalitarian social context.

Sherwood Lingenfelter elaborates on this "way of life" model, creating from it a tool to describe cultural change.[14] His development of this approach makes it possible to determine which of the ways of life are being followed in a given social setting.[15] By understanding this, we can assess the characteristics of an organization or a given social setting within a culture and understand how to bring about change within that group. Drawing on his descriptions (and adding our own thoughts in this area), we will discuss the five ways of life in detail, offering insight on how to create a plan for change in a specific cultural setting.

Egalitarian Society

As the word suggests, egalitarian societies stress equality. Individuals in an **egalitarian society** are group-oriented. Leaders are chosen among equals and generally do not have many resources at their disposal to do their work. They mingle with other groups in their societies and are usually indistinguishable from others in their patterns of dress, language, and standard of living. These leaders' influence comes from their ability to persuade others, not from any institutionalized authority that they possess.

> **EGALITARIAN SOCIETY**
> A group-oriented society marked by similar status levels; often considered closed to outsiders.

What is clear in such societies is who belongs in them and who does not. Becoming a group member is a lengthy process. In extreme cases, individuals from the outside cannot join; the only new members are born into the group. When outsiders are admitted to such societies, they must go through extensive training regarding how they should behave and the values they should hold. Individuals who do not accept the group's rules of behavior and values are confronted and dismissed. The Amish and a few other extremely conservative Protestant denominations represent egalitarian groups in the United States. Certain clubs also fall into this category.

Individualistic Society

In an **individualistic society**, the central theme is freedom of choice and the autonomy of individual members. Individuals can choose to stay in the society or leave at will. They also can choose their own codes of conduct within the society (most variations are accepted) and feel little obligation to conform to the expectations of others around them. Leaders garner their power by making exchange agreements with individuals. These agreements are temporary and must be renewed on a regular basis.

> **INDIVIDUALISTIC SOCIETY**
> A society based on freedom of choice and the autonomy of its individual members.

Throughout their time in leadership, leaders must constantly demonstrate why associating with them is valuable for the members of the group and why they are better equipped to lead than others. When these leaders die, there is no guarantee that their authority will be passed on to others. The new candidate for leadership must win the support of the people, just as the predecessor did.

An organizational example of this type of social context can be found in many real estate agencies throughout the United States. Highly successful agents often align themselves with a local agency through which they achieve the best return on their investment of time. Their exchange agreements with the agency relate to the percentage of profit they can keep from a sale and the percentage they share with the agency. Some cooperation occurs among agents, but there is no great incentive for work sharing, since agents are paid individually. A sales commission that must be divided between several agents can mean fewer profits for all.

> **HIERARCHICAL SOCIETY**
> A structured society in which individuals function at different levels or in different categories with dissimilar status.

Hierarchical Society

Another type of social context is a hierarchy. **Hierarchical societies** are quite structured, with each individual categorized according to the level in which that person functions. Rules of behavior govern their access to individuals from other levels, the way they communicate with them, and the type of information that can be shared. Hierarchical societies lack rules

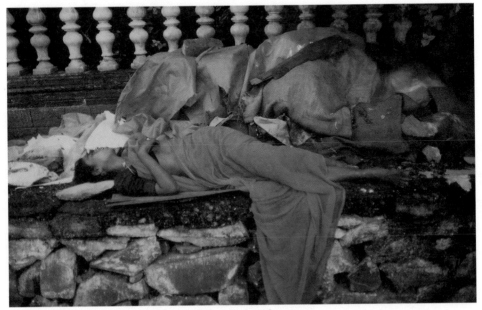

In India, the "lowest" levels of society often live on the streets.

regarding who can join and who can leave. Entrance and exit procedures may exist, but the borders are quite porous. Little about their behavior or appearance distinguishes those inside such societies from those on the outside.

When co-author John Johnson was still in graduate school, he worked part-time in the main administration building of his university. Occasionally, he was called on to move boxes for secretaries and administrators. He noted that the main office building functioned like a hierarchy, a society of many levels, something that was clear to everyone who came into the building. Individuals in higher levels of the organization had more spacious work areas than those in the lower levels. Everyone in the organization had a title and individuals seldom did one another's jobs, working instead at what they were trained to do. Those in higher positions of authority often were addressed by titles, whereas those with less authority were called by their first names. All of these factors are characteristic of a hierarchical society.

Fatalistic Society

Thompson, Ellis, and Wildavsky have categorized a fourth type of society as fatalistic.[16] We usually think of fatalism as a belief that things are fixed in advance and that human beings are powerless to change them. A **fatalistic society** does not embody this philosophy so much as it describes a particular type of society characterized by highly structured levels. What distinguishes a fatalistic society from a hierarchical society is that in addition to societal levels, a fatalistic society also has clearly defined boundaries. It is not easy to gain admission to or leave this kind of society.

FATALISTIC SOCIETY
A highly structured society that is difficult to enter or leave.

The U. S. Marines can be seen as an example of a fatalistic society. Not only do the Marines have clearly defined levels (ranks such as captain, general, etc.), they also have boundaries that make it difficult to enter and leave the society. When people join, they discover that there is much more involved than merely expressing a desire to join (all that some organizations require). Getting in takes months of intense training, which includes how to act like a Marine and how to relate to those above you in the organization. Marines discover that individuals at different levels are to be addressed in a specific way and not merely by their first names. The penalties for desertion are severe. Like the Marines, most military organizations are fatalistic societies.

Most cultures include hermits, those who choose to live alone.

Autonomous Society

The fifth type of social context is known as autonomy.[17] Individuals or groups who wish to withdraw from all other societies and live by themselves usually choose to form an **autonomous lifestyle.** From the hermits of ancient times to present-day survivalists, people have chosen to live separated from others. Many choose to live in the wilderness, having as little contact as possible with the larger society around them and creating ways to sustain themselves in order not to be dependent on that society. While many succeed in limiting their contact with others, complete isolation is rarely possible.

Autonomy is distinct from the other four "ways of life" because it does not involve interaction with others. Instead, it focuses on avoiding interaction. Throughout history and in many different cultures, individuals and groups have selected this path, choosing to resist all types of societies or to leave them altogether. In doing so they sacrifice the benefits of being part of the wider society, but avoid its obligations

> **AUTONOMOUS SOCIETY**
> Individuals or groups who live separated from the larger society and who have little or no interaction with others.

as well, including the need to conform to social expectations and submit to those in authority. In times of rapid social change, some individuals choose the autonomous lifestyle to avoid the stresses societal change places upon them.

A Present-Day Comparison: The United States and Japan

In the introduction to this section on social contexts, we mentioned that all these "ways of life" can be present in any culture. However, societies usually reflect a dominant pattern, emphasizing certain ways of life above others. Many business organizations in the United States often select the individualistic quadrant or the hierarchical quadrant as their pattern of choice. In individualistic organizations, membership in the organization is based on short-term contracts with other members of the organization. Levels are de-emphasized, the top person in the organization may mingle with others (with everyone on a first-name basis), and individuals are free to leave at will. Some organizations do emphasize hierarchy, but this is usually with the expectation that individuals can come and go at will. In both individualistic and hierarchical organizations, the group aspect is often weak, and lifetime membership in the organization is rarely guaranteed. The organization's commitment to its members is conditional, based on the quality of their work.

> Societies usually reflect a dominant pattern, emphasizing certain ways of life above others.

In contrast, Japanese business organizations generally prefer the fatalistic way of life because it demonstrates a greater orientation to the group than the American hierarchical structure does. In Japan, organizations are often committed to individuals for life, regardless of their performance. Poor performers are retrained and retained. The rationale is that even in difficult economic times, the Japanese corporation seeks to keep its people so that they will be available during times of economic growth.

THE FIVE WAYS OF LIFE AND CHANGE

How does this theory of the five ways apply to change? One example occurs when individuals become dissatisfied with one quadrant (e.g., hierarchical, individualistic, etc.), choose to leave, and then become part of a subculture that represents another quadrant. The Amish and Mennonite communities in the

United States have a regular stream of defectors, eager to cross the "border" to the outside world. In the same way, individuals who grew up in very individualistic environments are sometimes attracted to a more communal way of life, along with its shared resources and values. We saw many examples of this in the United States during the 1960s and 1970s, when young people from wealthy suburban homes joined communes or converted to conservative, group-oriented faiths.

A Flock of Starlings

Why do individuals choose to leave one type of society and join another? Individuals from cultures in which society is highly structured and bound by tradition (fatalistic) often long for more opportunity to make their own choices about life. In highly individualistic societies, such as the United States and Western Europe, individuals often feel challenged by and unprepared for the many choices they have to make. For example, individuals in group-oriented societies long for privacy, while those in more individualistic quadrants (hierarchical and individualistic) experience loneliness. Some of the world's loneliest people occupy retirement homes and apartment complexes in the United States and Western Europe. One testimony to this is the ballooning number of personal ads placed in newspapers, as well as the booming business in online matchmaking services.

Although individuals may leave one quadrant and join another, Thompson, Ellis, and Wildavsky believe that all of these ways of life will continue to exist. None are in danger of losing all their adherents and becoming extinct. These authors compare the process of change to a flock of starlings, which has the ability to remain seemingly in the same position overhead for

People today increasingly have an opportunity to join other quadrants or ways of life.

several minutes at a time. In doing so they do not fly in circles, but rather fly in a pattern that fills four quadrants. The only thing that keeps the flock from moving away is the fact that individual starlings are constantly shifting positions within the flock, exchanging places with starlings in other quadrants. If they stopped moving, they would fall to the ground, and if they assumed a fixed formation, they would not be able to stay in one place. They also do not all move to one quadrant and crowd each other out.

In the same manner, the five ways of life remain intact. Many individuals leave one way of life and join another, while a disenchanted few choose the hermit existence, withdrawing from community altogether.[18] People move from one quadrant to another; this keeps a society and the world from having only one "way" of life.

The Five Social Contexts and Organizations

The Thompson, Ellis, and Wildavsky approach is useful in understanding individuals and organizations. If we can assess into which quadrant an organization fits, we can predict to some extent how leadership is exercised, what tensions exist in the organization, and how individuals may wish to change.

In his study of change at the University of Lenin, co-author John Johnson discovered that a change in the economy of Ukraine caused many individuals within the organization to move from one quadrant to another.[19] When Ukraine was a part of the former Soviet Union, a professor's living costs were subsidized with low-cost housing, almost free transportation, and even free vacations. In this way the hierarchy of the university was maintained. Deans, rectors, and others in administration were feared and respected, their authority guaranteed. Nearly all professors belonged to the Communist Party, which demanded group loyalty as well. Individuals were expected to attend regular sessions and maintain a sense of community among themselves.

When Ukraine became independent, it lost much of its funding for education. Professors began to find part-time jobs in addition to their work at the university. As capitalism crept into the country, the part-time jobs began to pay well, much better than the professors could make by teaching at the university. Consequently, the authority of those above them eroded. Membership in the Communist Party declined sharply, as well, and the university soon became a very individualistic place.

CHANGE THEORIES AND THE STREET HAWKER IN KIEV

How does all of this apply to the backpacking marketer in Kiev, who was introduced at the beginning of this chapter? If he adopts an evolutionary approach to change, he might believe that his mission is to win converts to his ideas, thus leading them to a higher level of development—presumably the lofty one he occupies himself. If he applies the approach of Franz Boas (the individualistic approach to change), he will realize that in order to bring about change, he must study the language and understand the cultural patterns of those who surround him. The functional approach would lead him to be cautious. Suppose everyone on the square accepted his ideas. How would this affect their communities? Would the change be positive or negative for them? At the time of his marketing speech on the square, Ukraine's economy was fragile, requiring families to pool their labor in order to survive. Some individuals even abandoned their families to serve some interest group, leaving other family members to suffer the consequences.

Change theorists would accept the backpacking hawker's presence on the square as legitimate, even normal. But they would point to other efforts to change society as well. New signs promoting Coke abounded throughout the city, a product unavailable only a few years before. Adherents of Eastern religion promoted their message on the square, as did proponents of other ways of thinking. Ironically, as the nineties progressed, new ways of thinking became less appealing; many moved back to the Communist Party and the Orthodox Church, returning to their previous beliefs.

As important as it is to understand the process of cultural change, we need specific strategies with which to bring it about. We will discuss some of these in the next chapter, narrowing our focus to examine change in organizations and individuals. In this way we can explore how to exercise influence in a given setting.

KEY CONCEPTS

autonomous society
egalitarian society
evolutionary change model
fatalistic society
fieldwork
functional change model
hierarchical society
individualistic change model
individualistic society
interactionist change model
symbolic change model

QUESTIONS FOR DISCUSSION

1. Which of the approaches to change discussed in this chapter best describes how cultural change happens? Why do you feel this way?

2. Revisit the description of the five ways of life. Which way of life do you feel is most prevalent in your culture? Which is most prevalent in your organization? Give examples (and perhaps stories) to support your view. How might this model help you understand cultural and organizational change?

3. How might the knowledge you have gained in this chapter help you impact your world?

ENDNOTES

1. Robert Greenleaf, *Servant Leadership: A Journey into the Nature of Legitimate Power and Greatness* (Mahway, NJ: Paulist Press, 1991), 21, quoted in Robert Quinn, *Deep Change: Discovering the Leader Within* (San Francisco: Jossey-Bass, 1996), 218.

2. Helen Deresky, *International Management: Managing Across Borders and Cultures* (Upper Saddle River, NJ: Prentice Hall, 2003).

3. Gary P. Ferraro, *The Cultural Dimensions of International Business,* 4th ed. (Upper Saddle River, NJ: Prentice Hall, 2002), 19.

4. Lewis Henry Morgan, *Ancient Society* (New Brunswick, NJ: Transaction Publishers, 2000); originally published in 1877 by Henry Holt and Company.

5. Richard Nelson, "Understanding Eskimo Science," in *Annual Editions: Anthropology 01/02*, ed. Elvio Angeloni (Guilford, CT: McGraw-Hill/Dushkin, 2001), 70-72.

6. Gerald Leslie, Richard Larson, and Benjamin Gorman, *Introductory Sociology: Order and Change in Society* (New York: Oxford University Press, 1991), 3-11.

7. Daniel G. Bates, *Cultural Anthropology* (Boston: Allyn and Bacon, 1996).

8. Thomas Hylland Eriksen, *Small Places, Large Issues: An Introduction to Social and Cultural Anthropology* (Sterling, VA: Pluto Press, 2001), 22.

9. For a thorough treatment of Douglas's approach in this area, see her book, *Purity and Danger: An Analysis of the Concepts of Pollution and Taboo* (New York: Praeger Publishers, 1966).

10. Michael Thompson, Richard Ellis, and Aaron Wildavsky, *Cultural Theory* (Boulder, CO: Westview Press, 1990).

11. George Spindler, "The Transmission of Culture," in *Education and Cultural Process: Anthropological Approaches* (Prospect Heights, IL: Waveland Press, 1987).

12. Robert Layton, *An Introduction to Theory in Anthropology* (New York: Cambridge University Press, 1997), 98.

13. Mary Douglas and Aaron Wildavsky, "The Border is Alarmed," in *Risk and Culture: An Essay on the Selection of Technical and Environmental Damages* (Berkeley and Los Angeles: The University of California Press, 1983).

14. Sherwood Lingenfelter, *Transforming Culture*: A Challenge for Christian Mission (Grand Rapids: Baker Books, 1992).

15. This is a descriptive, qualitative approach to understanding cultural environments and is not intended to provide proof with statistical certainty in these areas.

16. Thompson, Ellis, Wildavsky, *Cultural Theory*.

17. Ibid.

18. Like the starlings, all cultures are in a constant process of change. Culture is described as "always in disequilibrium, always on the move, never exactly repeating

itself, always having a definite shape, yet never staying the same shape . . . yet no single shape has material permanence." From Thompson, Ellis, and Wildavsky, *Cultural Theory*, 86. In this model, cultural change is not necessarily destructive, but rather provides balance, equilibrium, and variety to any given society.

19. John S. Johnson, "Culture Change and Educational Leadership in Kiev, Ukraine" (Ph.D. diss., Biola University), abstract in Dissertation Abstracts International (1996).

CHAPTER FIVE

Understanding Organizational and Personal Change

A Kenyan graduate student in one of our courses was part of a nonprofit organization's effort to distribute food in Ethiopia. He had been sent to a part of Ethiopia in which traditional ways of doing things were highly revered. For these people, tradition applied not only to their lifestyles, but also to the production of food. They insisted on growing crops in the traditional way, rather than moving to more productive forms of agriculture. As a result, the food supply was insufficient, eventually resulting in a famine in the

Some cultures may not survive if they hold on to traditional ways of life.

region of the country the student was visiting. Everywhere he looked, children were dying from hunger. As he visited a local family, the mother walked him around the room, pointing out the members of her family who would die soon if food was not made available.

The student had been given money by the relief organization to buy a large quantity of food. However, the government operated the only stores in which it could be purchased. When he tried to buy food, the storekeeper asked for a bribe before he would sell to the student. The student complied and purchased the food. As he told us later, paying a bribe in this case was a matter of moral principle. He felt it necessary to do whatever was needed to keep the children from starving.

TROUBLING ISSUES

It is clear from this story that major changes are needed at every level of this local system. Any change in society must involve change in both individuals and organizations. In this case, because local farmers have not adopted more effective practices, children are dying from lack of food. A local businessperson is so unconcerned about the problem that he withholds food, demanding a bribe in addition to the food's actual cost. Because it allows such corruption, even the government is part of the problem. We can raise many troubling questions regarding the organizations and individuals in this story—questions about issues that are common around the world. Those involved in agricultural production could change the course of events by adapting to more efficient practices. That still might not be enough. Even if there were plenty of food in the region, a greedy employee could stop it from being distributed to those in need. Changing one segment of the culture will not make a difference when the culture needs systemic change in all segments involved in the problem.

> Changing one segment of a culture will not make a difference when the culture needs systemic change in all segments involved in the problem.

This chapter will provide some models of organizational and individual change. It will offer some ideas on where and how to begin, as well as some tools to make it happen. These tools are proven instruments, capable of bringing about positive results for the problems we described in chapter 3. To this end, this chapter

TABLE 5.1	
UNDERSTANDING ORGANIZATIONAL AND PERSONAL CHANGE: CHAPTER OVERVIEW	
ORGANIZATIONAL CHANGE	**PERSONAL CHANGE**
Understanding Organizations	Components of Personal Change
Bringing About Change in Organizations	Changing Individual Attitudes in Organizations

will cover organizational aspects of change, including structural, human resource, symbolic, and political perspectives. Then we will review a critical dimension of change—the impact that individuals can have within organizations.

THE ORGANIZATIONAL DIMENSIONS OF CHANGE

An Opportunity Lost

Effective change not only involves culture, but the organizations within a culture as well. Every culture is comprised of organizations, whether these organizations are highly structured or more loosely knit. In order to be lasting, effective cultural change must transform society by working through its organizational components. An example of this can be seen in the former Soviet Union. For many years, freedom-loving individuals throughout the world hoped that greater openness would come to this region. In the early 1990s that hope became a reality. Under the leadership of Mikhail Gorbachev, the nation began to consider new ways of thinking about economic issues. Religious persecution stopped and the Soviet Union was open to ideas and products from the outside world.

This new openness in society included an appetite for everything from Coca-Cola to pornography. Educational institutions were asking for input and the new government was receptive to new ideas. There was a receptivity to religion as well. However, the rest of the world was not fully prepared for what was happening in the Soviet Union. Cold War attitudes lingered in the world's governments, preventing them from forming partnerships of trust. Local Soviet

The former Soviet Union experienced the benefits and problems of opening its society to outside influences.

educational institutions that desired reform could not pay foreign specialists for their input. The developed nations of the world were still investing their budgets into Cold War defense, leaving little money to bring about organizational reforms.

The change in the country's government did draw the attention of interest groups around the world. They soon arrived on the scene in droves. But rather than focus on institutional reform, their emphasis was on immediate results. Foreign businesses wanted to see a quick return on investments and gave less attention to long-term economic growth. Humanitarian organizations looked for conversions to *their* ways of thinking. These involved a broad spectrum of causes, including environmental advocacy, women's rights, and evangelical Christianity. Modern crusades were an especially popular method of reaching those whose interest in religion had been rekindled. However, in many cases, local religious leaders were not consulted about how to conduct these campaigns or whether they even should be held. Sadly, little funding was allocated by the sponsors to support Eastern Orthodox Christianity, the historic faith of the region.

By the mid-nineties, Western businesses had opened shops in many cities. Students could obtain an education locally, thanks to the formation of private universities. But, overall, the immense local interest in things new had begun to subside. Interest groups had made some converts, but the openness to change was faltering. A chance to make a substantial difference was evaporating because little attention had been given to bringing about change in the local institutions of government, religion, education, and law. Had Christians, for example, tried to bring about change in local organizations, they might have created a context supportive of Christian values in the Soviet society. Instead, an opportunity was lost.

Understanding Organizations

Lee G. Bolman and Terrence E. Deal encourage us to view organizations through the eyes of an artist.[1] Artists see reality, reframe it in a creative way, and reproduce what they see. Four different artists may paint the same sunset and produce remarkably different pictures of the same reality. It is clear that they

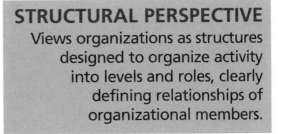

STRUCTURAL PERSPECTIVE
Views organizations as structures designed to organize activity into levels and roles, clearly defining relationships of organizational members.

viewed the scene in different ways. As we look at their pictures, we enter into their worlds, seeing the sunset ourselves in four different ways. In like manner, Bolman and Deal encourage us to look at organizations from four different perspectives.

The Structural Perspective

To view organizations through a structural perspective means to see them as structures designed to organize activity into levels and roles. The **structural perspective** sees organizations in terms of clearly defined relationships with little ambiguity for organizational members. Those at every level of the organization know what their jobs are and to whom they should report. They are specialists in their work, with few others in the organization capable of doing it as well. At least five assumptions undergird this structural perspective:

"I reported to the vice president of finance until someone discovered it wasn't a dotted line at all... just some spilled coffee."

Source: Copyright © 1995 by Mark Litzler. Reprinted by permission of Mark Litzler.

1. Organizations exist to meet established goals and objectives.

2. Organizations work best when rationality prevails over personal preferences and external pressures.

3. Structures must be designed to fit an organization's circumstances (including its goals, technology, and environment).

4. Organizations increase efficiency and enhance performance through specialization and division of labor.

5. Problems and performance gaps arise from structural deficiencies and can be remedied through restructuring.[2]

Clearly Defined

One company that exemplifies the structural perspective is McDonald's. Both co-authors have witnessed the opening of McDonald's restaurants in several countries. Upon entering these restaurants, they found the food and food preparation processes to be very similar to McDonald's restaurants they had patronized in the United States. The way local franchises are structured varies little around the world. Every restaurant has clearly defined roles and a number of management levels, including a regional director, restaurant manager, assistant manager, and staff employees.

HUMAN RESOURCE PERSPECTIVE

Views organizations as meeting human needs; particularly capitalizes on the fit between the organization and its members.

Individuals who view organizations through the structural perspective believe that in order to bring about change, the organization must be restructured. Positive change may involve eliminating levels, creating new roles, or adapting the structure to its business environment.

The Human Resource Perspective

A second way to view organizations is with a human resources perspective. From the **human resource perspective,** organizations exist to meet human needs. Building upon Abraham Maslow's model of human needs, a human resource theorist believes that the organizations should meet many, if not all, the defined needs. (See Figure 5.1.) The following assumptions underlie the human resource perspective:

1. Organizations exist to meet human needs rather than the reverse.

2. People and organizations need each other. Organizations need ideas,

energy, and talent; people need careers, salaries, and opportunities.

3. When the fit between individuals and the system is poor, one or both suffers: individuals will be exploited or will exploit the organization, or both will become victims.

4. A good fit benefits both. Individuals find meaningful and satisfying work, and organizations receive the talent and energy they need to succeed.[3]

From this point of view, positive change involves creating a better match between individual and organizational needs. Do individuals have areas of need that are not being met? Does the organization need services it is not receiving? If the answer to either question is yes, a human resource theorist would point to the need for positive change.

Unmet Needs

The film *Joe Versus the Volcano* offers a fictional example of unmet needs. For four years, Joe goes to work, doing a job that he finds distasteful and boring. He meets his need for variety by reading books at his desk, doing so without the knowledge of the organization. Because of the mismatch between employee and organization, the organization also receives little benefit from Joe's services. When he is misdiagnosed with a terminal illness, he quits, realizing that life is too short

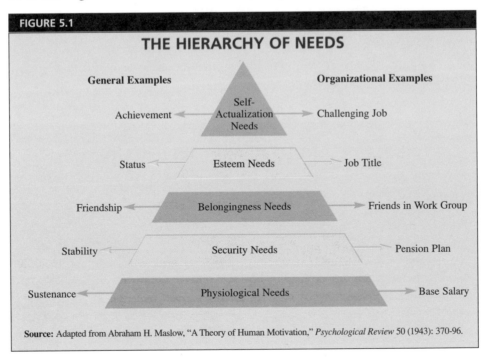

FIGURE 5.1

THE HIERARCHY OF NEEDS

General Examples		Organizational Examples
Achievement	Self-Actualization Needs	Challenging Job
Status	Esteem Needs	Job Title
Friendship	Belongingness Needs	Friends in Work Group
Stability	Security Needs	Pension Plan
Sustenance	Physiological Needs	Base Salary

Source: Adapted from Abraham H. Maslow, "A Theory of Human Motivation," *Psychological Review* 50 (1943): 370-96.

to be wasted in this way. He later learns that the diagnosis was false and that he is in perfect health. However, he chooses never to return to the organization.[4]

The Symbolic Perspective

SYMBOLIC PERSPECTIVE
Views organizations as places to help people find meaning through symbols, ceremonies, and stories.

Meaning, faith, and belief are important from a symbolic perspective. What is important is not what happens, but what it symbolizes. Symbols, rituals, and stories provide meaning for an organization and help to explain the decisions it makes. (See Table 5.2.) The **symbolic perspective** views organizations according to the following assumptions:

1. What is most important about any event is not what happened, but what it means.

2. Events have multiple meanings because people interpret experience differently.

3. In the face of uncertainty and ambiguity, people create symbols to resolve confusion, increase predictability, provide direction, and anchor hope and faith.

4. Many events and processes are more important for what is expressed than for what is produced. They form a cultural tapestry of secular myths, rituals, ceremonies, and stories that help people find meaning, purpose, and passion.[5]

TABLE 5.2

SYMBOLS THAT HOLD MEANING IN ORGANIZATIONS

Keys: Who can carry them? Who can use them? Who must be asked for permission?	Offices: What size is the office? What amenities does it have?
Parking Spaces: Whose parking space is closest to the office? Whose is reserved?	Stories: What stories are repeated often in the organization?
Company Cars: Who can use them? For what purposes can they be used?	Rituals: Meetings important not because of what is accomplished, but for who is there and who is not there.
Myths: Truths the organization holds about itself that individuals outside the organization may or may not believe. (Example: We are the best in our field.)	Decorum and Architecture: In what type of facility is the organization housed? What characterizes the décor? What types of pictures hang on the walls?

The Bronzed Typewriter

From a symbolic point of view, creating change involves respecting treasured symbols in an organization and mourning their loss if they are removed. An interesting example of this comes from the newspaper industry. U.S. newspapers hit a stumbling block when they tried to make the transition from typewriter to computer. Having a reporter write a story on the computer keyboard was a timesaving and much more efficient process of getting the story "to press." Material could be edited, typeset, and printed in one smooth process. However, getting reporters to *use* the new technology was not easy, as they preferred typewriters and were accustomed to producing their stories in this way.

One newspaper installed computers but found that getting stories out was actually taking longer. The publisher and managing editors began to suspect that reporters were writing the stories twice—creating the story on typewriters and then retyping the story on computers. They tried a number of initiatives, including redesigning the department's structure and providing training for computer usage, but nothing produced the desired results. The publisher became very frustrated. He had spent time, energy, and money to get reporters to take advantage of a more efficient system, but training, restructuring, and even threats all had failed.

Hired to assess the situation, a human resource consultant decided to focus on the symbolic aspects of the problem. He took a typewriter to a local metals specialist and had it bronzed. He then organized a party in the newsroom, presenting the bronzed typewriter to one of the most influential reporters in a ceremonial, symbolic fashion. In subsequent weeks, efficiency improved dramatically. Reporters gradually stopped using the typewriters and began to write on the computer keyboards. Management realized that the old rituals had provided meaning they were unaware of. When these symbols were replaced, they had to be mourned and buried before the new ones could become part of the culture. The consultant provided the appropriate "funeral and resurrection."[6]

The Political Perspective

The **political perspective** sees organizations as political arenas in which individuals, coalitions, and interest groups clamor for attention. It does not attribute organizational politics to individual selfishness or incompetence, but assumes that interdependence, differences, and scarcity will produce political activity,

POLITICAL PERSPECTIVE
Views organizations as political arenas in which individuals, coalitions, and interest groups compete for the organization's scarce resources.

regardless of how they are handled. The political perspective asserts that:

1. Organizations are coalitions of various individuals and interest groups.

2. There are enduring differences among coalition members in values, beliefs, information, interests, and perceptions of reality.

3. The most important decisions involve the allocation of scarce resources; i.e., who gets what.

4. Scarce resources and enduring differences give conflict a central role in organizational dynamics and make power the most important resource.

5. Groups and positions emerge from bargaining, negotiation, and jockeying for position among different stakeholders.[7]

When Everyone Loses

An example of the political perspective involves the 1986 launching of the space shuttle Challenger. One minute after takeoff, there was a massive explosion in the booster rockets. Millions watched around the world as the space shuttle and its crew were destroyed. Later analysis of the tragedy revealed that a failure of the synthetic "O" rings in the booster rockets caused the explosion. The booster rocket engines had been furnished by the Morton

In the political perspective, individuals try to achieve their own objectives.

The Challenger tragedy was an example, in part, of an internal power struggle in NASA.

Thiokol Corporation, a manufacturer of solid propulsion motors. Thiokol had sole rights as the contractor that provided the space shuttle rocket fuel engines. On the evening before the launch, a group of Thiokol engineers pleaded with their supervisors and NASA officials to delay the launch. It was unusually cold in Florida and they feared that the cold weather would cause a failure in the "O" rings that sealed joints in the rockets' motors, causing them to explode.

Three important groups struggled for power in the decision to launch. Executives at NASA needed the launch to proceed in order to boost NASA's popularity in Congress, where it was in danger of losing support. Thiokol's management team listened to its engineers, but its position as the sole provider of rocket fuel engines was at risk. The engineers could have brought about positive change had they been able to find ways of garnering greater influence within the organization. In the end, they lost to other groups that commanded more power and resources in the project.[8] This power struggle resulted in the deaths of seven and the suspension of the space program for two and a half years.

Bringing About Change in Organizations

As the Challenger tragedy underscores, one way to bring about organizational change is to recognize the kinds of power organizational members use to meet their goals. (See Table 5.3.) In an organizational sense, an individual's power is the ability to influence others. There are a number of different ways to bring this about.[9]

TABLE 5.3	
TYPES OF POWER IN ORGANIZATIONS	
Position Power	Expert Power
Reward Power	Reference Power
Coercive Power	Resistance Power

Position Power

One of the most common forms of influence is **position power.** This is the power invested in someone because that person holds an office; therefore, the authority is inherent in the position itself. Being president, CEO, or director carries with it certain rights. Followers may not care for the person who fills this role, but they will follow that person's leadership because of the authority implied in the leadership title.

> **POSITION POWER**
> The power invested in one who holds a position of authority in an organization.

The use of position power usually does not require a great deal of explanation or persuasion. Staff members are expected to follow the orders given by the boss. When the officeholder's term is up (or if the officeholder is assigned to a different role), the power is automatically transferred to the new officeholder. The person leaving the office cannot take this power along, as one would take personal effects to a new office. The new person must have full authority to do the job required of the office.

Reward Power

Anyone associated with money in an organization has some degree of reward power. **Reward power** is inherent in those who are able to do good things for others in the

> **REWARD POWER**
> The power invested in one who distributes compensation or other nonmonetary rewards to others in the organization.

organization. Individuals who distribute monetary rewards in an organization are usually thanked, whether or not they had any role in deciding the amount of the compensation or who should receive it. As such, reward power often is subtler than position power.

Nonmaterial rewards are generally valued as well. The editors of local publications use reward power when they decide who should be featured in the publication. In addition to public recognition, other kinds of rewards within organizations include well-located offices, prestigious parking places, and access to better equipment than others in the organization.

Coercive Power

Coercive power is the ability to force someone to do something, whether or not that person wishes to comply. Individuals with coercive power at their disposal often make the mistake of thinking that the application of coercive power

The application of coercive power does not necessarily result in people wanting to do what they initially are forced to do.

COERCIVE POWER
The ability to force someone in an organization to do something, even against that person's will.

will result in people *wanting* to do what they must initially be *forced* to do. Unfortunately, this is not the case. People forced to respond in a certain way generally will not choose to respond that way—if given the opportunity to choose.

Coercive power often is used in military organizations and prisons. In these organizational environments, individuals do not have a say in decisions and must do as they're told. Refusal to obey results in an escalating series of punishments determined by those in authority.

Expert Power

Expert power can be used by those who possess knowledge or skills which others need and do not have. This power increases if the expertise is scarce and if it is essential to carrying out the functions of the organization. Some examples include accountants in a financial services organization, intensive care nurses in a hospital with a shortage of nurses, or a cable television technician in a market with many new subscribers. Any specialists that are difficult to replace (and needed) can exert influence in this way.

EXPERT POWER
The power invested in someone who has expertise that is scarce in the organization.

In the technology boom of the 1990s, many computer specialists enjoyed the benefits that expert power brings. The IT industry did not have enough of them to go around. Many computer specialists commanded high salaries, could come and go to work when they wished, and were not scolded when they broke their company's rules. Work history was not important, nor was an individual's interpersonal skills. All was forgiven by companies who did not have the specialists they needed. These specialists commanded great expert power.

"Keys" to Success

Professionals are not the only individuals who can command expert power. Some may be familiar with the story of a janitor who had worked in a factory for many years. He kept track of all keys to the factory, using a system that hardly anyone else understood. After many years of faithful service, he began to feel that management was treating him unfairly. He became very dissatisfied and decided to quit without notice. One morning, the supervisor of morning shift arrived to discover that all of the building's doors were locked. He went to the key room, but could not decipher which keys went to which doors. After trying to guess for three days (while the company lost money), the janitor was hired back, this time as a consultant. He was paid three times what he had received before and was given the honor accorded to an expert—which, in fact, he was. He had benefited from expert power.

Reference Power

Those who are well connected can apply **reference power.** It is used in introductions, for example, when one individual recommends another to someone that she or he may know. A number of years ago, co-author John Johnson had an extended meeting with a top education official of the country in which he was presenting a seminar. This visit provided a wonderful opportunity to understand higher education in this country and to understand more about the local leadership. This dialogue was possible not because of who John was, but through the recommendation of a longtime friend of the official (who was also John's friend).

REFERENCE POWER
The power invested in someone who can recommend or positively reference someone else.

Chinese people throughout the world know how to apply reference power well, using a method referred to as *Guanshi*. In many cases, it works like a preferred trading partners network, taking the place of a credit reference system (which does not exist in many of the countries involved). Individuals who are approved by the network can buy and sell without credit or background checks.

Resistance Power

Resistance power is the power of refusal. While generally it is not difficult to overcome one person who is resisting authority in some way, the task becomes more challenging when resisters unite with others of like mind. Their positions in the organization are not important. Those in low-status positions can become formidable foes if they choose to exercise power in this way. Organizations can be brought to a halt (and sometimes are) if a sufficient number of employees choose to resist.

RESISTANCE POWER
The power of refusal vested in those who unite with others in the organization to achieve an objective.

Typical examples of resistance power involve students who agree not to attend class, factory workers who go on strike, and airline pilots who refuse to fly. A few years ago the pilots of Lufthansa, Germany's national airline, refused to fly on one given day every week because of a labor dispute. The airline lost millions of dollars because of this action, but could not force the pilots to go to work on that day. Since they could not replace all the pilots, the company was forced to allow them to carry out this action, and the pilots gained their objectives.

Organizational Power in Cross-Cultural Settings

Our work in international training leads us to believe that different cultures vary in the kinds of power they use, depending on the values that they cherish. Citizens of the United States often depend on position power. They have high regard for an office and respect the nameplate on the door. This is also evident in their high regard for the rule of law.

Co-author John Johnson came to a different conclusion during his research in Ukraine. He found that the executives he studied needed more than position power. Their effectiveness was not due to their positions (which were significant), but to their extensive network in government, business, and education. When the organization could not provide them with the authority they needed, they were able to fall back on the network (reference power) they had developed over the years. Individuals without this type of a network were not valued and could not compete in the business environment.[10]

Citizens who have experienced repressive governments are not as likely to attempt the use of resistance power. Managers of global companies in China can bear witness to this fact, where the greatest challenge many of them face is the development of human resources. Companies from around the world who work in China are trying to develop individuals who will solve problems, take risks, and resist traditional ways of thinking. But

In the United States, individuals often are given responsibilities that they must handle alone.

they find that getting individuals to take any risks at all is difficult to accomplish. Years of oppression have left their mark, especially on those who lived during the leadership of Chairman Mao. In those days, resistance was punished, sometimes by death—and old ways are difficult to change.

In a similar way, citizens in countries with strong social hierarchies also can have trouble changing. Co-author Boyd Johnson observed in many Asian cultures a deeply embedded deference to authority figures. If their leaders resist change, it can be quite difficult for others to alter how things are done. It is essential in these cases to understand the cultural dimensions of change, and how power is used in different societies.

THE PERSONAL DIMENSIONS OF CHANGE

Thus far we have focused on the importance of cultural and organizational change. Yet to truly bring about change, we also need to understand how it occurs on an individual level. How can we facilitate change as it relates to individuals in organizations? We should take two steps:

1. Identify those whose attitudes we would like to change, and

2. Assess their relationship to us.

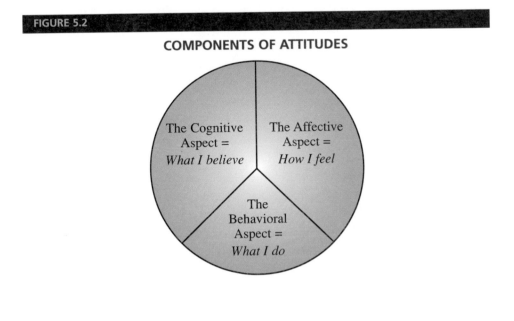

FIGURE 5.2

COMPONENTS OF ATTITUDES

The Cognitive Aspect = *What I believe*

The Affective Aspect = *How I feel*

The Behavioral Aspect = *What I do*

Components of Personal Change

Attitudes are important in the change process. When looking at attitudes, we can identify three components or dimensions, all of which are involved in the change process:

1. The cognitive aspect (what I *believe* about something).
2. The affective or emotional aspect (how I *feel* about something).
3. The behavioral aspect (what I *do* based on what I believe and how I feel).

Reinforcing the Message

For a person's attitude to change about something, all three dimensions must be involved. For example, when co-author John Johnson was in his twenties, he did not understand the value of physical exercise. His family did not view vigorous exercise as important. Since he was homeschooled from grades three through twelve, he was not involved in sporting events. Later, while working on his master's degree, he took a class on spiritual and physical wholeness. The professor, a medical doctor, impressed on John the value of physical exercise as a way to relieve stress. John's patterns of exercise did not change after the course, but the doctor/professor's words made a deep impression on his thinking (cognitive). His eventual friendship with the doctor caused him to think more frequently about what he had taught him, and to view his opinions about exercise in a positive light. The message was reinforced as John continued to meet other individuals who felt that exercise was important and who practiced it in their everyday lives. The emotional component of his attitude was beginning to change.

A few years later, John completed his schooling and moved to Europe. He enjoyed his job, but the stress of cross-cultural living began to take its toll. He remembered his doctor friend and some of the other individuals who emphasized the importance of exercise. He became so convinced of its importance that he bought the best bicycle he could find. During the most stressful times of his year, he carefully budgeted his time in order to ride trails on the new bike. From that day forward, mountain biking, roller-blading, and skiing became an important part of his life. The behavioral part of his attitude had changed.

In this example (changing attitudes about exercise), the affective component was key. When attempting to change the attitudes of others, we often focus our efforts on the cognitive aspect—what they believe. However important this aspect is in changing an attitude, it is not the component most likely to resist change. Most change efforts fail in the affective (or emotional) arena.

Changing Individual Attitudes in Organizations

The first step to take when attempting to bring about change in an organization is to focus on who can partner with us. Who this might be depends on the cultural context. In some cultures it may be the oldest individuals in the organization. In others it will be those in senior positions. After the decision makers have been identified, the next step is to negotiate with them. In order to be effective in negotiating, we should first define their relationship to us.

Peter Block envisions negotiation as a grid, with a quadrant for different individuals within an organization.[11] Two continuums are used to assess their relationship with us. We asses them based on our ability to agree with them and on the level of trust that exists between us. There are five possible positions in regards to their relationship with you. (See Chart 5.1.)

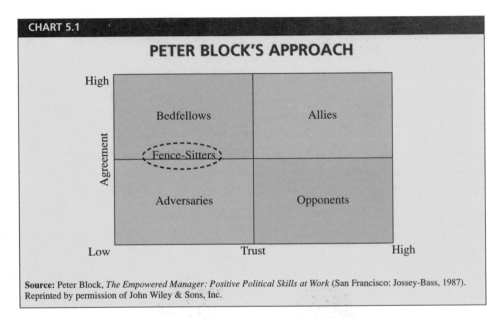

CHART 5.1

PETER BLOCK'S APPROACH

Source: Peter Block, *The Empowered Manager: Positive Political Skills at Work* (San Francisco: Jossey-Bass, 1987). Reprinted by permission of John Wiley & Sons, Inc.

In the diagram we can see that the upper right-hand quadrant is for our *Allies*. With them, we experience the benefits of both agreement and trust. The bottom right quadrant is for our *Opponents*. With opponents, we experience trust but not agreement. The upper left-hand corner is reserved for our *Bedfellows*. Bedfellows generally share our beliefs (and agree with them), but there is little trust shared. Individuals in the bottom left corner are our *Adversaries*. This can be one of the most difficult groups to deal with. We do not agree with them and do not trust them. *Fence-Sitters* can also be difficult (on the line between bedfellows and adversaries). These are persons who never seem to take a definitive stance. We can meet with them, discuss the issues, and think we know what they believe. But when it is time to stand for what they believe, fence-sitters falter and never seem to know who they are.

After identifying the decision makers that we need to influence, we then can place them in the appropriate quadrants. Who are they in relationship to us and/or to our team? How much agreement and trust do we share? Are they allies, opponents, bedfellows, fence-sitters, or adversaries? Where they fit in the model helps determine how to relate to them.

Make the Most of Allies

ALLIES
Decision makers with whom we experience agreement and trust.

The **Allies** in our organization can be a great source of strength. It is important to identify who they are, develop channels of communication, and share our strategy and vision with them. In the process of doing this, ask for their support. The strength and caring we receive from them can give us the courage to face our opposition. Because we trust them and agree with them, they help to fill us with positive emotional energy when difficult meetings and conflicts drain us.

We can be open with our allies. We should express our doubts and fears about projects (or ideas) and ask for their input on how to proceed. We need to share our vision with them and reaffirm their interest in the things we share.

Opponents can force us to rethink our assumptions.

Value Opponents

How can **Opponents** be valuable to us if they do not agree with us? The key element is trust. Opponents can ask probing questions, push for answers, and help think through the project or idea we are promoting—all the while in the safe environment of trust.

> ### OPPONENTS
> Decision makers with whom we experience trust but not agreement.

It is easy to overlook the value of opponents. If we are looking for confirmation of our vision's validity, we may not find it in opponents. It takes courage to listen to those who do not agree with us. But because we trust them, we need to listen to them carefully, consider what they say, and rethink our own strategy in light of their input.

Listen to Bedfellows

Bedfellows may agree with us, but we still may not trust them. The positive aspect of this relationship is the area of shared agreement. The negative aspect

> ### BEDFELLOWS
> Decision makers with whom we generally experience agreement but little trust.

is the inherent suspicion we have about them. In some cases this is due simply to the newness of our relationship (as with individuals we have not known for long). In other cases it results from our history with them, including negative memories and a possible record of offenses.

Bedfellows need to know exactly what we want from them. We should also ask them what they expect from us. Our role is to listen to them and help them realize that we are trying to understand them. We should resist any temptation to be defensive and to be influenced by past wrongs. We must forgive them for their lack of trust in us, realizing that they too have been subject to pain and loss of trust from others.

Deal with Fence-Sitters

Organizations probably complain more about **Fence-Sitters** than any other group. Like bedfellows, we do not share trust with the fence-sitters around us. But the problem goes deeper, as fence-sitters are reluctant to take any definitive position at all.

Fence-Sitters often have excellent interpersonal skills. They feel that careful listening will help any problem go away. They know how to frame conflicts in a way that makes them disappear, at least for the moment. We

FENCE-SITTERS
Decision makers about whom we are uncertain regarding agreement and trust issues.

present our vision to them, but at the end of the meeting it is difficult to know whether or not they have made a decision. We may learn later that in meetings with others they were ambivalent on the issue, choosing to take a noncommittal position. When we need their action or support, they fail to come through.

Fence-Sitters often are motivated by fear of failure. They may want to take action but are afraid of the risks involved, including the risk of offending others in the organization. This leaves them by necessity in a neutral stance, unable to fully commit to any project with any degree of risk. They may espouse officially sanctioned ideas, but refuse to endorse anything with a shadow of question.

Fence-Sitters must be asked to state where they stand. They should be encouraged to express opinions without being judged for what they say. Gentle pressure must be applied in an effort to persuade them to take a more definitive position. They must be called to commitment and asked what we would need to do in order to gain their complete support.

A fence-sitting boss may not seem like an asset, but may be a blessing in disguise. The fact that this individual does not take a stand may free us to take a path of our own choosing. Our wish for the fence-sitter to take a strong stand may actually be an expression of our own dependency and need for safety and approval. This type of environment can help us to clarify our own priorities and give us an opportunity to develop the extra strength we need to succeed.

Negotiate with Adversaries

Adversaries require much time and energy. We do not share agreement with them nor do we share trust. Because of this, successful negotiation is difficult to accomplish. Unfortunately, much of the time we place individuals in this quadrant before they may actually belong there.

ADVERSARIES
Decision makers with whom we do not experience agreement or trust.

The first question to ask about individuals that we perceive to be adversaries is whether or not they actually belong in this category. In many cases, we place names in this quadrant based on past experiences with them or the perception of others. People should only be placed in this quadrant if all attempts to negotiate with them have failed. Before we reach conclusions, we should share with them our vision and give them an opportunity to respond. This in itself can be difficult, as we may be afraid to share information with those we do not trust.

It is important to make every effort to communicate with adversaries. We should listen to them and attempt to restate their position in a neutral way. It is important to identify any contribution we may have made to the lack of trust, or to the adversarial relationship that we feel. We should leave the meeting without making demands. When the vision has been presented, it is up to them to decide what their response will be.

Not all adversarial relationships can be changed. In some cases, it is better to seek a separation and choose other individuals with whom to work. In the case of an adversarial subordinate (who does not respond to negotiation), we may need to replace that person with someone else. The situation with an adversarial superior can be more difficult. Working for someone we do not trust (and who does not share our vision) can be torture. After attempting to negotiate, there may be no real solution to the problem. We live in the hope that they will choose to leave the position or that another opportunity will open up for us.

Communication is essential in dealing with adversaries.

Summary

Defining the characteristics of our relationships with others can help us understand their attitudes and enable us to work with them where they are. As we identify those who share our views (our allies), we can strengthen the support needed to bring about change. By discussing ideas with our opponents, we refine our beliefs and are better prepared to face whatever opposition may come. Our bedfellows sharpen our relational skills, and fence-sitters teach us tolerance. Our adversaries stretch us in many ways, helping us to refine our vision for change, to reassess our priorities, and to wait patiently for the outcomes we need.

ORGANIZATIONAL AND PERSONAL CHANGE: MAKING IT HAPPEN

KEY CONCEPTS

adversaries
allies
bedfellows
coercive power
expert power
fence-sitters
human resource perspective
opponents
political perspective
position power
reference power
resistance power
reward power
structural perspective
symbolic perspective

As we understand the poverty, hunger, and spiritual needs of our world, we realize the critical importance of positive change. Any successful attempt at change must include strategies for changing both organizations and the individuals that serve within them. Can we actually accomplish such initiatives? While some organizations are resistant, experience has shown that change efforts can make a difference, both within the organizations and the cultures that surround them. Successful initiatives never happen on their own, but are crafted by effective change agents, individuals who resist the self-serving tendencies of their culture to bring about good in the world. We will meet seven such individuals in chapters 6 and 7. These are people who assessed the needs of their world, developed their skills, and made a difference.

QUESTIONS FOR DISCUSSION

1. In the organizations with which you are associated, what kinds of power do you see individuals apply? Give specific examples.

2. What kinds of attitude changes have you experienced in the last three years? Ten years? Describe how these changes occurred. Who or what brought them about?

3. Draw two lines on a piece of paper (or a whiteboard), dividing the paper into four squares of equal size. Using Peter Block's approach, analyze your personal relationships in your organization. Who are your allies, adversaries, opponents, bedfellows, and fence-sitters? How might this model impact the way you relate to them? How can you work with them to bring about positive change in your organization?

ENDNOTES

1. Lee G. Bolman and Terrence E. Deal, *Reframing Organizations: Artistry, Choice, and Leadership* (San Francisco; Jossey-Bass, 1996).
2. Ibid., 40.
3. Ibid., 102-03.
4. *Joe Versus the Volcano*. Directed by John Patrick Shanley and produced by Teri Schwartz. (Hollywood: Warner Brothers, 1990).
5. Bolman and Deal, *Reframing Organizations*, 216.
6. Lee G. Bolman and Terrence E. Deal, *Modern Approaches to Understanding and Managing Organizations* (San Francisco; Jossey-Bass, 1984), 40-216.
7. Ibid., 163.
8. Malcolm McConnell, *Challenger: A Major Malfunction* (Garden City, NY: Doubleday, 1987), 7.
9. Adapted from Jerald Greenberg and Robert A. Baron, *Behavior in Organizations,* 6th ed. (Upper Saddle River, NJ: Prentice Hall, 1997), 405-09.
10. John S. Johnson, "Culture Change and Educational Leadership in Kiev, Ukraine" (Ph.D. diss., Biola University), abstract in Dissertation Abstracts International (1996).
11. Peter Block, *The Empowered Manager: Positive Political Skills at Work* (San Francisco; Jossey Bass, 1987), 138-60.

CHAPTER SIX

Understanding the Practice of Change in the United States

WHAT PEARL DO YOU SEEK?

An ancient tale describes a mythical king who decides to send his son on a sacred mission to Earth. The purpose of the journey is to find and bring back the "pearl that resides in the sea." Anxious to take on this challenge, the prince leaves the kingdom with great resolve. But the moment he arrives on Earth (also the moment of his birth), he forgets both his purpose and origins. Drawn to the attractions around him, he comes to believe that living life on Earth is his only purpose. He marries, has children, and enjoys life's pleasures, all the while remaining in a state of spiritual forgetfulness.

On his son's fortieth birthday, the king sends him a message: "Remember your mission, seek the pearl and return." The prince does not listen; he is too immersed in his life. The king sends the message again, this time in a different form. Again and again, he tries to get his son's attention, calling him back to what he should be doing with his life. Over time, the son begins to understand and listen to the messages. As he does, he realizes their urgency and meaning. After much hesitation and a few false starts, he answers the call, finds the pearl, and returns to the kingdom.[1]

This ancient tale can have present application. What "pearl" should we be seeking? Some people seem to understand this "quest" early on, but for many others, understanding comes later in life. Whatever the specifics of the message, one fact is clear. Fulfilling our vision will create positive change for those around us. Among other things, the pearl we are seeking should involve bringing good to our world.

But how can this be done? In this chapter and the next, we will introduce people who have used the strategies outlined in this book to bring about change in their worlds. By describing their lives and work, we hope to show that change is indeed possible, and that a variety of methods can be used to bring it about. Although the needs are very great, one person *can* make a difference.

This chapter will profile four individuals who have brought about change while residing in the United States. Chapter 7 will focus on three people who have effected change while residing in other countries. Like John Woolman (in chapter 4), these seven individuals demonstrate a strong commitment to positive social change, motivated by their faith and the desire to make a difference with their lives. We know these people personally[2] and have witnessed their work firsthand.[3]

"Serve at Home": Words from Mother Teresa

Several years ago, co-author Boyd Johnson visited one of Mother Teresa's ministry sites in Calcutta. He was deeply moved by what he saw and encouraged to continue his own efforts to help the poor. He learned later that her ministry had affected many others in the same way. Several even offered to leave their countries of residence and help her with the work in Calcutta. But rather than tell them to relocate, Mother Theresa encouraged them to return home and minister *where they were*—where they could better understand the needs, speak the language, and make a meaningful difference. Practical and wise, she realized that many people can make a difference in meeting the world's needs while living in their home countries.

The people profiled in this chapter have changed the world from a base in the United States. Barb and Ray Schulz ministered from Indiana, Gwendolyn Robinson worked in Cincinnati, and John Flores served near Chicago. The following is a summary of their work and the strategies they used to bring about change.

TABLE 6.1			
CHANGE AGENTS	RAY AND BARB SCHULZ	GWENDOLYN ROBINSON	JOHN FLORES
Cultures and Subcultures Targeted	Developing countries in need of medical support The medical and business community in the United States	Culturally diverse areas of Cincinnati	Culturally diverse areas of Indiana and Illinois
Skills Employed	Management and medical expertise	Teaching, leadership, cross-cultural bridge building	Leadership skills
Strategies Utilized	Short-term mission trips Mobilizing the U.S. medical community to meet needs	Giving hope Accepting differences Teaching diversity	Support for families Acceptance of diversity Networking with community leaders

RAY AND BARB SCHULZ: MEDICINE AND MANAGEMENT

Every year, various nonprofit groups sponsor short-term medical clinics in a number of developing countries. During the week they are in town, volunteer doctors, nurses, and dentists help the people of these countries with their health needs. It is a unique form of giving, as most of those served could not obtain help in any other way.

In the last decade, Barb and Ray Schulz have managed short-term clinics like these, impacting approximately 75,000 people. Most of their clients are poor, uninsured, and unable to visit a doctor. Barb and Ray set up their clinics in local churches, cooperating with the religious network already in place and ensuring a continuity of support to those with needs after the volunteers leave.

Ray and Barb Schulz

As a nurse, Barb manages the medical aspects of the team while Ray, a businessman, carries the administrative load. Because the work is grueling, many team leaders lack the stamina to stand up to the challenge. As a result, several initiatives such as theirs have been plagued with chronic management problems. That doesn't seem to be a problem with the Schulz clinics. World-class physicians, who are accustomed to giving the orders, take directions from Ray. His years of executive experience lend credibility to what he says. This makes the difference, bringing harmony to teams that could be fractured by egoism and self-direction.

This couple's skills did not evolve by accident. A number of important incidents in their lives helped to develop the leadership skills they employ today.

Ray Schulz: Innovation and Self-Service

From 1970 to 1990, the way Americans purchase gasoline changed forever. In the early seventies, most Americans bought their gas at small stations and allowed someone else to pump it for them. If a restroom was even available, it was accessible only to customers (you had to ask for the key). A typical gas station ("service station") offered auto repair services, dedicating a majority of the floor space to this work. The space accessible to customers was limited and was sometimes used to sell soft drinks and a few snacks or candy bars.

All this changed in the eighties and nineties. In today's "gas station," scores of different refreshments are available. Customers pump their own gas and go elsewhere for car repairs. Counter clerks often provide local directions, but would hardly be expected to fix anyone's car (or have time to do so). In rural communities throughout America, these revamped gas stations now are referred to as convenience stores and have become a sort of community meeting place for surrounding residents. While gas is still available (self-serve, of course), it almost seems that there are more services inside than outside.

One of the men most responsible for this change in the Midwest is Ray Schulz. Ray promoted these innovations as president of Speedway Petroleum, a wholly owned subsidiary of the Marathon Oil Company.

Mississippi, Missouri, and Marathon

Born in Mississippi, Ray later attended Evangel College in Missouri. There he met and married Barb. From the beginning it was clear that she would be a major influence in his life. After a short stay in Florida, they moved to Muncie, Indiana, which was the city Barb called home. Ray began working as a loan officer, then began his studies at Ball State University.

After graduating from Ball State, he accepted a position with Marathon Oil, working in their offices in Indianapolis and Louisville. Several promotions later, he completed executive training at Harvard University and was appointed the president of Speedway Petroleum, a new division of Marathon. He moved the Speedway headquarters from Ohio to Indianapolis and began experimenting with self-service stations.

Other Speedway executives questioned Ray's initial efforts and his innovative approach. But the bottom line revealed a profit. In one location, Ray borrowed $75,000 from another budget fund to add food and services to the station, a move that could have cost him his job. It soon became clear that he had invested the money well. In less than a year, the station's income had doubled.

As Speedway acquired new stations, their service bays were transformed into customer space. Cash inflows increased as refreshments, chips, and coffee were offered. Fast food made its debut as well. The Midwest convenience store was born.

Barb Schulz: Nursing as Ministry

Born in Indiana, Barb grew up and attended school in Muncie. She was an excellent student, something that did not escape the notice of others at school and at church. As Barb finished high school, she was offered scholarships to

Barb in Latin America.

three colleges: Indiana University, Ball State University (in Muncie), and Evangel College in Springfield, Missouri. She selected Evangel and began the pre-med program there, a decision that would prove to be providential. She met Ray and within three years they were married. As he began his studies at Ball State University, she worked as a secretary.

When Ray began his career, Barb helped to support their family by working as a kindergarten teacher, which allowed her the time she needed to continue her homemaking responsibilities. But as the children grew older, she felt called to a career involvement as well. She responded to the call by enrolling in Marymount Hospital School of Nursing near Cleveland, Ohio, where Ray was working. A year later she graduated as a certified L.P.N. She received her R.N. in 1982 and completed her bachelor of science degree in nursing (B.S.N.) in 1984. As they moved around the country, her interest in nursing continued, and she eventually earned a master's degree in nursing as well. She accepted a faculty position at Indiana University Purdue University Indianapolis (IUPUI), which offers one of the best nursing programs in the state.

Nursing, Pulling Teeth, and a Trip to Ecuador

In 1988, at the invitation of her daughter Shauna, Barb spent two weeks in Argentina applying her nursing skills and assisting in dentistry. She was struck by the extensive need she witnessed and decided to participate in a future ministry trip.

The next year found her in Ecuador, ministering to the poor in the barrios of Quito. One mother was so desperate to get medical attention for her baby that she stepped out of the line and put her baby's face into the barbed wire fence. The child's bleeding face guaranteed her a place at the front of the long line of sick people, some of whom the team would not have had time to treat. Scenes such as this affected Barb deeply, helping her to realize how much she was needed and solidifying her decision to return.

On the next trip to Ecuador, Ray accompanied Barb and Shauna. As a

This medical mission uses available transportation.

nonmedical member of the team, at first he felt out of place. A dentist on the team asked him to work with him to pull teeth, as the dentist had a problem with his arm and there was no one else to help. Ray knew nothing about dentistry and nothing he had learned at Speedway had prepared him for this task. After praying for a miracle, he agreed to assist.

Within a week, Ray's fears had vanished. He not only learned to pull teeth, but learned to do it well. The dentist he worked with was so pleased with his support that he jokingly bestowed on him an honorary doctorate of dentistry in front of the other members of the team. As Ray returned to the United States, he realized that he was learning to be open to new things.

Barb and Ray continued their involvement with medical teams during their free time. With his expertise in providing service to customers (as he did by creating the convenience store), he became the systems manager, keeping the doctors, patients, and support staff at peak efficiency. For her part, Barb headed up the medical side of the team, sorting out medicines and responding to triage questions about care.

A Call to an International Ministry

In March 1992 Ray went with a medical mission team to Eastern Europe. While there, he found that he could not sleep past 4:00 A.M., so he took advantage of this as an opportunity to pray. Early in the morning on his last day in the region, he sensed that God would change the direction of his life. He felt specifically that he should accept an early retirement from Speedway and become a full-time director of teams on medical mission trips.

Astute businessperson that he is, Ray gave God some conditions to fulfill. He asked that the medical director of the mission would sit beside him on his return flight and ask him to accept a full-time role in the ministry. He stipulated before God as well that his house would sell, and that Barb would share his vision for the future.

As he began the flight home, the medical director was nowhere near. Ray began to doubt the vision, feeling he had been led astray. The plane landed in Helsinki, Finland, then took off again for the United States. This time the medical director sat across the aisle and began to talk to him. As time passed, he crossed the aisle, sat beside Ray, and asked him to take on the full-time responsibility of medical team director for their ministry.

Back in the United States, Ray presented the plan to Barb. She showed no surprise when he explained his vision. She had felt drawn toward the same vision in prayer a few days earlier. As Ray had prayed in the early morning hours, she had sensed God leading them into full-time service during the evening hours in Indiana. Comparing notes, they realized that God was giving them the same vision at the same time. Shortly afterwards, Ray took an early retirement from his job at Speedway Petroleum. Together, Ray and Barb began to lead medical teams internationally, making an impact on a number of communities around the world.

The Work Continues: The Ministry Today

Barb and Ray Schulz have shared their faith in over fifty medical and dental ministry trips. The specialists who travel with them on these trips take time away from their practices and are not paid. They minister in the areas of eye care and dentistry, as well as general medical services. Each client receives a New Testament in his or her language and hears about Christ one on one. "It's so great to look out on a courtyard and see a person wearing glasses he has just received, reading the Bible in his own language," Barb says.

> "It's so great to look out on a courtyard and see a person wearing glasses he has just received, reading the Bible in his own language."
>
> Barb Schulz

During their time in the United States, Barb and Ray continue their ministry by training others to do what they have done. Barb serves as Director of the RNBS Completion Program at Indiana Wesleyan University. In the curriculum and with the professors of the program, she emphasizes the importance of care for the needy. Ray serves as a consultant to church and business leaders in the area of leadership.

Lessons We Can Learn

What can we learn from Barb and Ray? One thing is clear—they have understood the needs of those with whom they have come in contact and have made a difference in these people's lives. Like Franz Boas (chapter 4), they realized that they could not fully understand the needs from the reports of others. They decided to go out in order to understand the needs empirically for themselves. It would have been easier not to go, merely continuing what they were doing, making money, supporting their children, and enjoying a life of comfort. But Barb and Ray fought against the current, resisting the emphasis on achievement so endemic to our culture (as described in chapter 2). Their time is valuable, but they give it away generously. In so doing, they make a difference in the lives of others.

Today's affordable and efficient transportation systems allow them to visit needy areas of the world, then return to the United States to continue their work. They make every effort not to disrupt the functioning of the communities they serve, connecting what they do with local medical personnel and area churches.

TABLE 6.2	
BARB AND RAY SCHULZ: LESSONS AND NEEDS	
Lessons to Learn	Busy professionals can make a difference in the world.
	The pressures of materialism in American culture can be resisted and overcome.
	All of our skills can be used to bring about positive change in the world.
World Needs Addressed	Helped to provide health care for those unable to provide it for themselves.
	Mobilized the resources of the American medical community to meet the needs of the world.

GWENDOLYN ROBINSON: CULTURAL BRIDGE BUILDER

In September 1950 the Cincinnati school district had a serious classroom shortage, especially the city's west end. At the same time, other sections of Cincinnati were not affected by this shortage, most notably those areas with more affluent residents.

Washburn Elementary School near Laurel Homes (a Cincinnati Public Housing Development) was especially hard hit. In order to alleviate the crowding, classes for kindergarten, first, and second grades were conducted in the Laurel Homes basement. It was an ordinary basement, utilitarian and unattractive. Uncovered pipes lined the ceiling and an odor of dampness hung in the air. In spite of these conditions, Gwendolyn Robinson has many good memories of her days as a student there.

Gwendolyn Robinson and students

After three years of classes at Laurel Homes, Gwendolyn at last was given a desk at Washburn Elementary School—in a room above the ground. Four years later, she took the entrance exam for Walnut Hills, an elite college preparatory high school in Cincinnati's central eastside area. Four sixth-grade classes at Washburn took the test, but only four children were able to pass it. Gwendolyn Robinson was one of those four.[4]

Learning to Build a Bridge

As she progressed over the years at Walnut Hills, Gwendolyn realized that the environment in which she found herself was quite different from that in which she had grown up. She was one of only fifteen African American students in her graduating class. The remaining 285 students came from White, Asian, and Middle Eastern groups. This class was religiously diverse as well, including Protestant, Catholic, Hindu, and Jewish students. Her circle of friends became cosmopolitan, and she found herself visiting the homes of wealthy and culturally diverse families.

Gwendolyn's exemplary performance in high school won her a scholarship at the University of Cincinnati. In 1967, she graduated with a bachelor's degree in elementary education. Shortly before graduation, she began work as a teacher. She then completed her master of education in 1970.

"You'd Better Be Ready"

The sixth grade class at Windsor school came with a well-established reputation. Before accepting her assignment, Gwendolyn watched in dismay as the students did everything but throw their present teacher out the window.

"Are you going to be our new teacher?" one student asked. Gwendolyn tentatively nodded her head.

"Then you'd better be ready for us," he said.

She took this as a personal challenge. When starting day arrived, she was ready. She made it clear from the beginning that she was serious about helping the students learn. She continued with an active participation exercise that the class loved. They fell in love with her as well. She later would describe her involvement with this class as the best teaching experience in her life.

During her second year of teaching, a Chinese girl who spoke no English was added to her class. Gwendolyn planned every lesson with this child in mind, creating activities that enabled her to learn from the other children. It was a remarkable success story. At the end of only one year, the Chinese child was fluent in English. The barriers had been broken down between the two cultures. As they played with their Chinese classmate, the native English-speaking children learned a lesson in acceptance as well.

In the years to come, Gwendolyn would build many bridges between cultures. As a guidance counselor at Campbell Junior High School, she brought together the families of blue-collar workers and professionals. At Western Hills High School, she served as a counselor in a predominantly white school. As the first African American counselor to ever serve in the school, she had the opportunity to expose students to the rich heritage of her own cultural background. Barriers were broken down as individuals from Caucasian backgrounds came to appreciate other aspects of American culture, some they had never been exposed to in this way.

Building Bridges through the Arts

Gwendolyn's next position allowed her to emphasize something she had always loved. As an administrator (vice-principal) who coached artistic performance, she was given the opportunity to make the School for Creative and Performing Arts the first high school in the nation to conduct a play at the National Theater in Washington, D.C. The act of getting the cast to Washington

Change agents often must build "bridges" in order to help others.

was theater in itself, as three hundred students from diverse backgrounds made the 600-mile trip together in a caravan of buses. Their performance of *The Wiz*[5] won the hearts of the city's elite, including the mayor of Washington, who celebrated their visit with a parade in their honor. These and other learning experiences helped produce successful graduates, including Sarah Jessica Parker, Jeffrey Sams, Scott Moening, Todd Louiso, and other nationally known members of the performance community.

Building Bridges at Hoffman

In 1982, Gwendolyn was appointed the principal of Hoffman Elementary School. Most of the school's children lived in a depressed area of the city and were from single family homes, headed by women. Many of these mothers lived on public assistance and did not have jobs. Because of this, Gwendolyn had a vision of building bridges between this economically depressed community and the business community. In assessing the needs, she noted a direct connection between low-performing students and the kind of parenting they received at home. To address this need, she invited a psychologist to the school to teach parenting classes. These classes were designed not only to help the mothers, but also to increase support for the students at home.

> "Some of the brightest young mothers in our community were headed for dead-end careers."
> Gwendolyn Robinson

Gwendolyn's efforts did much to improve the economic standing of the school community as well. Gwendolyn later reminisced that "some of the brightest young mothers in our community were headed for dead-end careers." The framework she established helped those in need of vocational support to obtain the GED, write resumes, and perform well in interviews. A partnership with Western Southern Insurance assisted their children, while the Private Industry Council helped to ensure that those who applied for jobs had a chance to be accepted.

She also invited individuals who could model leadership to visit the school and participate in her bridge-building efforts. Some of these included Ken Blackwell (Ohio's secretary of state), the Reverend Fred Shuttlesworth, and the gospel Grammy winning Charles Fold Singers. Less than exemplary partners were included as well, among them prisoners from the local jail. They supported the school by repairing it on weekends, making their contribution when the students were not around.[6]

Building a Bridge to the World

In the early 1980s, a focus group was formed to study the influence of world languages on society. In addition to making students more marketable to the world, this group felt its study also might ease the racial tensions in Cincinnati by focusing the community on cultures that were less represented there. As a result of these deliberations, the Academy of World Languages was created to promote competence in less commonly taught languages for children in kindergarten through fifth grade. Rather than teach languages in a traditional way, this academy wanted to immerse children in the languages from kindergarten on. Non-language related courses (such as mathematics) would use this medium of instruction as well. The Cincinnati Bilingual Academy was founded at the same time for grades six through eight.

Learning different languages is an effective bridge-building tool.

In searching for someone to lead the new schools, the focus group had a number of important qualities in mind. They wanted someone from Cincinnati who understood the community well. They also were looking for someone who believed in the importance of learning languages and who could use the schools to build a bridge between Cincinnati's ethnic communities. In Gwendolyn Robinson, they found the person they needed.

These two schools became a forum in which different cultures of the city could meet and interact. The Parent Teacher Organizations of the schools brought families together from Russian, Chinese, Hispanic, and French backgrounds. Separate parent associations were organized for each language group as well, providing parents who spoke the same language a place to interact on their own.

The language schools served to connect Cincinnati with the world. A flag representing every country flew at the entrance of the school. A yearly international festival provided a context for this expression, where art, dance, cuisine, and other aspects of diversity were brought together. Schools throughout Cincinnati sent children to the event, thus increasing their international awareness.

In a country where different languages are seldom spoken, foreign visitors found an audience who understood them at the school.[7] Gwendolyn hosted delegations from all over the world, including mayors, ambassadors, and leaders in education from many countries.[8] Students from other countries came to study at the school, while students from the language schools traveled to study in other countries.

Over the years the school has had enormous influence. Around 2,500 language majors graduated between 1985 and 1999. Nearly all of them communicated comfortably in at least two languages, and some were fluent in three or four. These graduates went out across the globe as cultural bridge builders, spreading understanding and goodwill. Today, the values they learned at school are being spread around the world through their work as language teachers, international businesspeople, cross-cultural attorneys, and members of other professions.

Lessons in Building from Gwendolyn's Life

What can we learn from Gwendolyn's life? One lesson is clear: she made personal sacrifices to bring education to those who lacked economic and educational privilege. She looked beyond the ethnocentricity around her (as described in chapter 2) and built bridges to connect and celebrate all cultures in Cincinnati.

By helping Cincinnati's youth learn other languages, she sent them out around the world, building bridges wherever they went. Some have stayed in the United States, using their languages to communicate with the growing immigrant communities around them. As they promote understanding and acceptance, they help to prevent violence and discord.

Gwendolyn's work demonstrates the conflict approach to change. Cincinnati's social order was clear: those with wealth and position could obtain a good education; those without wealth and position could not. She helped those who were disadvantaged by the system confront it, overcome it, and prosper within it. In working with those who had resources, she helped them understand how to equip the less privileged. Her work with the city's youth sent them on to successful careers, giving them the skills they needed to lead, to articulate their views, and to support their own communities.

TABLE 6.3	
GWENDOLYN ROBINSON: LESSONS AND NEEDS	
Lessons to Learn	Teach individuals from different cultural backgrounds to understand one another.
	Build bridges between those who need support and those who can provide it.
World Needs Addressed	Understood the need for marketable skills to help the underprivileged provide for their communities and contribute meaningfully to the world.
	Focused on the need to accept, understand, and communicate with others.

DR. JOHN FLORES:
THE SAILING SUPERINTENDENT

East Chicago is not known for its sailing enthusiasts. But on any given summer day, some of its finest residents can be found cruising in sailboats across Lake Michigan, pushed along by the wind in their sails. On bright summer days, students of the city's high schools make their way to the shore to learn about sailing and water safety. In addition to their other instructors, John Flores, the school superintendent, sometimes sails with them. As one who helped create the curriculum, his passion is to expand the horizons of the city's youth, both cognitively and literally. Sailing across the waves, they learn about physics, teamwork, and weather. In the process, John also builds relationships with them, something he has done for years.

Dr. John Flores

Navigating the Neighborhood

Born in East Chicago, John Flores grew up in an African American part of the city. His parents were immigrants from Mexico, and John was the first of nine siblings to be born in the Chicago area. His early education (grades one through seven) took place in the local parish school. His mother, Conception, added to her otherwise heavy workload by exchanging work with the local Catholic parish to pay for his tuition and that of his other siblings. In addition, his father held two jobs, working a total of sixteen hours every day. With cooking and cleaning for nine children, his mother's role was just as demanding.

Mrs. Flores's investment in her children was destined to pay off. After graduating from high school, John attended Indiana State University to pursue a bachelor's degree. Over the next several years, he earned a total of four degrees, culminating with his Ph.D. in educational administration.

Well before completing his studies, John's career was already in motion. With schools all over the nation opening their doors to him, he made a deliberate choice to work in East Chicago. After serving in that community as teacher, vice principal, and dean, he became the principal of Central High School.

Central High students soon realized that their principal was available when they needed him, for he found them wherever they were. He walked the hallways frequently, socializing with students as he went. These "walks" involved much leadership activity—he helped to solve problems, answer questions, and air concerns.

Staying the Course in a Storm

While John was at Central High, something happened in California that affected the entire nation. An African American motorist named Rodney King was beaten by white police in Los Angeles. A videotape of this event shook the nation, especially areas with African American and Hispanic populations. Rioting occurred across the country, requiring urban schools to exercise unusual control and precaution. But at Central High, all was calm. As John later observed, "The expectation was that being a school with a diverse population, we would have riots and would experience other problems as well. We moved through the time with no repercussions at all."

One of the reasons Central High School stayed on course was John's concerted effort to support cultural understanding in the community. He

Navigating different cultures is a necessary skill for change agents.

encouraged ethnic dinners, clubs, and similar activities. In addition to designing Hispanic and African American curriculums, he created a supportive track for students from any background who entered the school as underachievers. The lowest performing eighty students were placed in small classes and given individualized instruction. Because John handpicked many of these white individualized instructors, he added a cross-cultural element to the program.[9]

Sailing in Other Seas

In 1996, John left East Chicago to become the principal of Maine West High School in Des Plaines, Illinois. As a predominantly white school, Maine West represented a new cultural context for him, one in which he had not served previously. His work there represented something new for the school as well, since he was the first member of a minority group to occupy the principal's office there.

John met the challenges with a community approach to leadership. He led by modeling, displaying a real interest in the 2,100 students that he served. He interacted with them, learned their names, and listened to them at lunchtime. He would later note, "I earned the right and respect of these students, since the majority of them had stereotypically viewed Mexicans in a different perspective."

> "I earned the right and respect of these students, since the majority of them had stereotypically viewed Mexicans in a different perspective."
>
> John Flores

Leading the school to new openness was not without its challenges. While approaching a group of students one day, John heard them speaking Spanish to each other in the hall. A teacher standing nearby who could not understand them was upset, noting that everyone "should speak English in this country." John took the teacher aside and explained that native speakers of a language sometimes choose to communicate in that language to provide a cultural "comfort zone" for themselves. The teacher accepted his explanation and soon came to realize that all children are valuable, no matter what language they speak.

In June 1997, the school board of East Chicago asked him to return and take up his responsibilities as school superintendent there. His work at Des Plaines had been salutary; parents, teachers, and students found it difficult to let him go.

Sailing at Home

As he began his job as superintendent, John realized there were challenges to face. As the school district with the highest poverty rate in Indiana, he knew that his job was unique. Around 56 percent of the students lived in single-parent homes, most of them headed by single mothers. Some homes in the district lacked even the standard amenities of running water, winter heat, and a refrigerator. These conditions put more demands on the students' schools, which needed to parent them, challenge them to grow, and play a role in their development.

John at work.

John's new job as superintendent involved the supervision of ten schools, including seven elementary schools, two junior high schools, and one high school. It was a culturally diverse community, with 52 percent of its students from native Spanish-speaking homes and 39 percent from African American homes. A growing Asian and Caucasian community was present as well. The mobility rate was high—a study of one school in the district showed that only 15 percent of the students who started school in kindergarten completed sixth grade in the same school system.

John's focus in the district has been to bring about positive change, both in the schools and in the community. He led the first "March Against Violence" in the community, pulling together religious, civic, and educational leaders in a combined focus to reduce crime. As a result, the amount of violence the community has experienced has been reduced by 24 percent in the last sixteen years. The degree of gang involvement also has been reduced. In 1986, 24 percent of the community's youth were involved in gangs, while today only 12 percent are involved. John started an academic league as well, which allows teams of children from different schools in the community to compete with one another academically, much as baseball and football teams do. He also initiated an underwater research center that attempts to recreate the natural habitat of the lake.[10]

These academic initiatives have paid dividends to the community. Around 79 percent of the district's high school graduates go on to college, up from a college-bound rate of 52 percent in the late 1980s. Some of those who study in universities outside the community will return (like John), contributing their new knowledge and making the East Chicago community a better place to live.

Lessons in Sailing from John Flores's Life

What can we learn from John Flores's life? As we reflect on his influence, the following lessons are clear.

"Expect It, Respect It!"

As a person who grew up in East Chicago, John knew the area well. Rather than leave after completing his education (as many of his peers did), he came back to help with the community's problems. Taking a functional approach, he could see some areas in which the community was not meeting the needs of its members. He worked within the system, thus improving education and decreasing violence.

> "All children cry the same, regardless of their cultural background. All people feel pain and similar emotions."
>
> John Flores

John's work also gives evidence of a conflict approach to change. He feels that cross-cultural interchange can be a positive experience, noting that many leaders do not promote diversity because they fear conflict and the domination of one cultural group over another. "We should view every cultural involvement as a positive experience," he says. His approach to diversity is expressed in the slogan, "Expect it, respect it." In accordance with this, the East Chicago schools respect different forms of communication and encourage children to speak to one another in their native languages.

John has consistently sought to understand the cultures around him. "All children cry the same, regardless of their cultural background," he notes. "All people feel pain and similar emotions." Fluency in Spanish and his desire to learn have facilitated John's efforts to better understand those in his community. He visits the schools under his care two to three times a year, encouraging parents, teachers, and principals to communicate with one another.

In a few years, the entire United States may mirror the diversity found in East Chicago and other urban areas. By emulating John's principles, individuals can produce cross-cultural change, both now and in the future.

TABLE 6.4	
JOHN FLORES: LESSONS AND NEEDS	
Lessons to Learn	Bringing about change begins at home.
	Communities function better when their needs are met (functional approach).
	Cultural conflict can be changed into cultural understanding.
World Needs Addressed	Economic needs: helped prevent inner-city poverty through parent programs and education.
	Helped to prevent violence by understanding the community's cultures and by providing alternatives to a life of crime (sailing and other school activities).

FACILITATING CHANGE FROM HOME

Individuals such as those profiled in this chapter help us see that positive change *can* happen in our world. From ordinary beginnings, all four of these people prepared themselves to make a difference. They stood against the negative aspects of their cultures, resisted discouragement, and overcame obstacles. Their lives exemplify a path we can take as well, seeing the needs around us and finding a way to address them.

As we will see in chapter 7, others are meant to take a different path of active involvement while living outside the United States.

QUESTIONS FOR DISCUSSION

1. To which of the profiles in this chapter do you most relate? In bringing about change, what lesson can you learn from the individuals profiled?

2. The individuals discussed in this chapter brought about change without moving away from their home country. To what cross-cultural environments do you have access today? What might you do to bring about positive change in these environments?

3. All of the individuals profiled in this chapter used their skills to meet specific needs that concerned them. Review chapter 3 and list three world needs that concern you. How might you use your skills to help meet these needs?

ENDNOTES

1. Adapted from Harry Moody, *The Five Stages of the Soul*: *Charting the Spiritual Passages That Shape Our Lives* (New York: Doubleday, 1997), 59-60.
2. All of the individuals profiled are personal acquaintances of at least one of the authors.
3. We have been granted permission to share the information in this chapter, which we obtained through personal interviews. These profiles have not been published before.
4. In Gwendolyn's life, education has always been a community affair, and her entire community encouraged her to excel. The Jordon home was full of books and her parents asked her often about her assignments from school. Other members of the community around her (a non-white area of Cincinnati) spurred her on. As she later noted, "Every neighbor knew your name . . . urged you to go on for more education." The day-to-day discrimination they experienced helped them realize the importance of education for their children.
5. *The Wiz* is a stage production derived from the book by William Brown, with music and lyrics by Charlie Smalls. Based on *The Wizard of Oz* by L. Frank Baum, *The Wiz* emphasizes cultural diversity.
6. Over a three-year period, great things happened at Hoffman. Professionals were invited to career days at the school, meeting students and encouraging them to pursue a higher education. Problems with discipline decreased dramatically as well. Parents found jobs, providing a better learning climate for their children. As a result, there were fewer behavioral problems to deal with when children were at school. Many of the students went on to Withrow, a high school for college-bound students.
7. Of course, different languages are spoken in the United States. However, in comparison to many countries, we lag behind in this area.
8. Among other visitors were mayors from Geifu, Japan, and Luishou, China, as well as civic leaders from Munich, Germany.
9. In addition to the personalized instruction they received, students were taken on learning expeditions that emphasized museums, architecture, and the great cultural riches of the Chicago area. The sailing course was introduced as well, an idea planted in John's mind by one of his professors. Since John could not afford to sail himself when he was young, he wanted young people in his school to have the opportunity to learn to sail. Around 80 students enrolled per semester in the program. In addition to being a great form of recreation, these students learned a new trade, landing jobs as yacht sailors in the Great Lakes region.
10. On February 29, 1999, a unique learning experience took place. East Chicago schools participated in a worldwide learning event. Children from seventeen countries were

learning underwater at the same time, united by international television screens that were present in each location. As a part of this experience, children from the East Chicago school district conducted an underwater assembly operation in their aquatics research center on the shore of Lake Michigan. Children from England directed the process of assembly, supervising the East Chicago students by television.

CHAPTER SEVEN

Understanding the Practice of Change in International Contexts

CHANGE AGENTS TO THE WORLD

On a recent trip to Africa, co-author John Johnson visited the source of the Nile River, which is Lake Victoria in Uganda. Lake Victoria is Africa's largest lake and the world's second largest freshwater lake. The water moving past John that day traveled from Lake Victoria north to the Mediterranean Sea, taking three months to complete its trip. It passed through Sudan and Egypt on its way, countries whose lifeblood depends on its nourishment.

A few hundred yards from the river's beginnings, the ashes of Mahatma Gandhi are buried in a vault. Although he loved his homeland of India, Gandhi chose not to be buried there. His best-known work occurred in India, but he also had lived in Africa for many years, advocating freedom from colonial rule. By being buried in Africa, he communicated that his concern for the world reached beyond his homeland with its many needs to other countries in the world

The individuals we feature in this chapter have brought about effective change while living in other countries. In their own unique ways, they have met the needs of the world. As important as it is to be a change agent at home, there are those—like Ghandi—who should serve in other environments as well.

TABLE 7.1			
CHANGE AGENTS	BOB YOUNG	GERALD BUSTIN	JUDITH D'AMICO
Cultures and Subcultures Targeted	Argentina, Brazil, Lebanon, Iran, South Africa, and the former Soviet Union	Papua New Guinea, Ukraine, Brazil, Fiji, and the Bahamas	Haiti, Alaska, and, Chicago's inner city
Skills Employed	Counseling and training counselors	Creative thinking and visionary leadership	Medical expertise and leadership skills
Strategies Utilized	Teaching at the university level Developing focus groups	Developing leaders Recruiting associates Raising money	Living with those in need Learning their languages Demonstrating love

DR. BOB YOUNG: INTERNATIONAL LISTENER

Dr. Bob Young

One of the dynamics of our world today is widespread, rapid change. Chapter 1 of this text explains how change has had a profound impact on nations, communities, and individuals. With the disintegration of some social institutions (such as families, villages, and tribes), people are left with no one to listen to them and nowhere to turn for support. This can be especially difficult for children. Among the kinds of support available to them are school counseling programs around the world. In the Middle East, a counselor has an especially important role— to support children in times of crisis, helping them adjust to the violence they witness and the reality of changing family roles.

Bob Young trained many of the counselors in the Middle East. Using the skills he carefully taught them, these counselors do their work, listening, caring, and supporting those in need. Some of his students train counselors themselves; others work as presidents of universities, respected professors, or national leaders in their fields.

Preparing to Listen

Born in Iowa, Bob grew up during the Great Depression. Like other families of the period, his parents struggled to make ends meet, and survived by eating milk toast (a budget combination of milk and bread). The difficult circumstances they faced inspired them to hope for better things for their children. With his bright mind and abilities, Bob began to fulfill his parents' dream.

After finishing high school, Bob attended the University of Iowa and enrolled in a bachelor's program in accounting. But World War II interfered with his plans. The Navy needed supply officers for ships at sea and decided that accounting majors would fit nicely into their plans. Hoping to serve his country, Bob enlisted in the Officers Training Program.

After a year of leadership training at the Amos Tuck School of Business Administration at Dartmouth College, he was shipped off to the Pacific, becoming Officer-in-Charge of an aircraft carrier. The pressures of the job were intense. Almost every day, kamikaze pilots targeted their ship. On one occasion, a Japanese plane was headed into the ship until a gunman shot it down at the last minute. Bob saw the pilot as he sped by and plunged to his death in the ocean.

Rescued from the Pit

The war took its toll on his men as well. One third of the crew were hospitalized and sent home with psychological problems. Bob managed to hold on to his sanity, but awoke every day with major questions about the meaning of his life. He experimented with different religions, all the time running from the fear that life had no meaning at all. When the war ended, he entered a deep depression, drinking himself to the point of intoxication almost every day.

After a three-day bout of drinking in the Philippines (on the island of Manikani in the Leyte Gulf), he found himself too drunk to walk home. Friends carried him to the ship, carefully avoiding contact with the men he commanded. He woke up the next day with a terrible hangover. He discovered that he had malaria as well. Like others in the military, he had contracted malaria at an earlier point during the war. He remembered to his shame that excessive drinking can cause malaria to return, and he felt that he was descending into an emotional and spiritual grave.

Later, Bob found a Gideon New Testament (with Psalms) on deck and began thumbing through its pages. Opening to Psalm 30:3, he read: "O Lord, thou hast brought up my soul from the grave: thou hast kept me alive, that I should not go down to the pit" (KJV). The Psalmist declared that God was the one who rescued him and kept him from descending into the pit. In prayer, Bob committed his life to Christ, becoming a new person. His malaria cleared up and he began to sense that his life had new meaning.

On his return from the Pacific, Bob stopped in San Francisco. He enjoyed the ambiance of the area and promised to return someday. After completing his degree in Iowa City, he enrolled at Stanford University, south of San Francisco. He earned a master of economics and then decided to attend Fuller Theological Seminary. As he began his courses there, he heard a speaker named Bob Smith at an Intervarsity Christian Fellowship camp. Smith highlighted the need for Christians in psychology, sociology, and the social sciences. Bob Young was challenged by this message and sensed a calling to a different vision. After only a year in the seminary, he headed back to Stanford. His friends at Fuller were suspicious of this change. Some felt he was leaving to "train in the world." Ignoring their opposition, he enrolled in a sociology doctorate program at Stanford.

Listening to Students at Stanford and La Plata

One of the groups that supported Bob during his years at Stanford was the Intervarsity Christian Fellowship. He encountered anti-Christian discrimination in the sociology program and decided to work full time for the student ministry.

"O Lord, thou hast brought up my soul from the grave: thou hast kept me alive, that I should not go down to the pit." Psalm 30:3, a Scripture pivotal to Bob Young's mission.

His role was to counsel and inspire students as they pursued their academic goals. After serving at Stanford for two years, Intervarsity offered him an assignment in Argentina. He soon found himself working at the University of Eva Perón in the city of La Plata south of Buenos Aires.

Riots and revolutions frequently interrupted Bob's work in Argentina. Three revolutions took place during his four years in Argentina, and each time the university shut down. This provided him with opportunities to help people in this stressful and unsettled environment. It also gave him time to travel and encourage students in other South American countries. On one trip to Peru, he befriended a young Peruvian named Samuel Escobar, a meeting that would prove to be providential. Through the support of Bob and other mentors he met through Intervarsity, Escobar's influence widened and grew stronger. He eventually became the International Director of the International Fellowship of Evangelical Students (IFES), the parent organization of Intervarsity Christian Fellowship and other student movements around the world.

> Riots and revolutions frequently interrupted Bob's work in Argentina. This provided him with opportunities to help people in this stressful and unsettled environment.

After four years in Argentina, Bob sensed that it was time to move on. He had helped to develop leaders who were now ready to direct much of the student activity on their own. Having worked himself out of a job, he decided to move to Brazil. There he organized student groups and continued his counseling and training of counselors. His philosophy there was similar to what it had been in Argentina: multiply his efforts through training others. As a result of this emphasis, he eventually felt he was no longer needed in Brazil as well. He returned to Stanford and completed a doctorate in educational psychology. After defending his dissertation, he married Inga and was invited to train school counselors at the American University of Beirut.

Listening to the Sounds of War

The remarkable aspect of Bob's assignment in Beirut was the wide range of influence it afforded his ministry. As a highly regarded university in the region, the American University of Beirut attracted students from all over the Middle East. Bob taught the best and brightest from Iran, Palestine, Egypt, and many other countries. After graduation they went back to their own countries, carrying the knowledge they had learned and the values imparted to them by a Christian professor.

Bob did a good deal of counseling in Beirut as well. Much of it evolved around issues raised by religion, especially conflicts between Christian, Muslim, and Jewish ways of thinking. The conflict vocalized in the sessions was soon to erupt in a more direct manner. He later realized that he was feeling the pulse of a coming war. One day in June 1967, as Bob and Inga were worshiping together, they read Micah 2:10: "Arise ye, and depart; for this is not your rest." With the current conditions of the nation, Bob sensed a prophetic ring to the verses.

For some time, he had been listening to the radio program "Voice of Israel" in Spanish about the growing tensions between Arabs and Israel.[1] The next day, he placed Inga and their children on a SAS flight that would start them on their journey to Denmark. It would prove to be the airline's last flight before the war. A few days later, the 1967 Arab-Israeli War began. Bob stayed to coordinate the evacuation of other Americans in the area. For about one week, he ran the rendezvous point for Americans at the university, barely escaping himself as the war started.

One of the students Bob met in Beirut was from Iran. He asked for Bob's resume and took it to the cultural attaché of the American Embassy in Tehran. Soon, Bob was interviewed by the Iranian government and asked to direct a guidance counseling center in Tehran, a city of eight million people.

Listening to Future Counselors in Iran

The Institute of Guidance that Bob directed was the only place in Iran where school counselors could be trained. As a part of the University of Teacher Education, it combined an academic emphasis with practical preparation in the field. For Bob and Inga, it was the beginning of a wonderful four years.

> At the International College of Insurance in Tehran, students in his class began to question him about his own view of human nature. Bob described his position from the Bible, describing man's sinful nature and need for salvation.

The ministry in Iran followed a similar pattern as the one in Beirut. Bob made many contacts with Muslims on the campus or in the classroom and invited them to his home. There, Inga provided warm hospitality and a culturally appropriate meal (taking into account the culinary restrictions of the

Bob and colleagues in the Middle East.

Islamic religion). As their children climbed up on the laps of the guests, barriers of culture and religion melted away. The family worked as a team, reaching others in a unique and heartfelt way.

In addition to his role at the Guidance Center, Bob taught students from all over the Middle East at the International College of Insurance in Tehran. As he had done in Beirut, Bob counseled students in the midst of a very tense context. Some of those with whom he and Inga had contact came under suspicion by the government. One of his students, an officer in the army, was questioned all night by government authorities, who suspected Bob of being an American spy.

Despite the opposition, there were great opportunities for sharing new ideas. On one occasion as Bob lectured in class, he referred to the famous educator Dr. C. Gilbert Wrenn and his view of human nature. Students in his class began to question him about his own view of human nature. Bob described his position from the Bible, describing man's sinful nature and need for salvation. It was to become one of his most popular lectures, one he was asked to repeat in several different situations.

Bob and Inga's efforts in Tehran led to the development of many new counselors throughout the country, scores of fruitful counseling sessions, and the initiation of a Christian school for missionary children. Among other activities,

Bob and Inga supported the work of a chapter of The Gideons International, which distributed Bibles throughout the country. Toward the end of their four years, Bob was hired by the mayor of Tehran to provide cross-cultural training to the youth of the city—yet another opportunity to meet needs that previously had not been addressed.

In later years a more conservative Islamic government came to power in Iran. Since that time, invitations to foreign professors have been slow in coming. To this day, no opportunities exist for individuals to do in Iran what Bob and Inga accomplished. However, some of his students went on to higher educational leadership and currently occupy some of the top leadership positions in the country. To protect their roles there, we will not discuss their ideological orientation, but it is enough to say that Bob's teaching and ministry had a great impact on their lives.

Fighting Discrimination in South Africa

From Iran, Bob and Inga moved to South Africa. As he took up his post as Chair of the Educational Psychology Department at the University of Natal, Pietermaritzburg, he began to realize how prevalent discrimination was throughout the country. Blacks and Whites were required to use different toilets and could not stay in the same quarters overnight. The government would not allow interracial meetings to be held unless separate toilets were provided for those represented! Many other rules prevented interaction between the two groups as well.

> As Bob spoke at Zululand University's commencement, he focused on the need for Christ to empower people. A few years later, voices such as his prevailed, and apartheid was banned from the country.

The Young family set about to break the rules, forming close friendships among the Zulus. As Bob spoke at Zululand University's commencement (something he had been forbidden to do), he focused on the need for Christ to empower people. A few years later, voices such as his prevailed, and apartheid was banned from the country.

The last twenty-five years of Bob and Inga's work have been invested in California, Ukraine, and Kazakstan. In California, Bob has trained counselors at the university level, preparing them to support others in their marriages and families. In Ukraine he has taught educational psychology, lived in a communist dormitory, and mentored people who became leaders in the International Fellowship of Christian

Students in Ukraine.[2] He taught in two universities in Kazakstan and helped to found a business college that spreads its influence to this day.

TABLE 7.2	
BOB YOUNG: LESSONS AND NEEDS	
Lessons to Learn	Learn to *listen* to individuals from other cultures and understand their needs. Train others to do what you do . . . your influence will be multiplied. Take time to prepare and use the expertise you have gained.
World Needs Addressed	Provided emotional support and coping skills in war-prone areas.

Lessons in Listening from Bob Young's Life

What can we learn from Bob Young's life? One of the most powerful statements it makes is the importance of listening as a ministry. Many feel called to speak, but few have the patience to listen. Bob never lacked for clients in his task, as someone who need his support was always around. He listened to expressions of hatred, love, anger, and desire for war, responding with the love of Christ in every situation. Inga's role was indispensable in this ministry, as she supported everyone they met through the ministry of hospitality.

> Bob Young listened to expressions of hatred, love, anger, and desire for war, responding with the love of Christ in every situation.

Through his professional skills, Bob became a part of local systems, entering doors that are seldom open to outsiders. He understood that the world was changing and this enabled him to equip individuals in the Middle East and elsewhere to adjust to these changes. As a friend, counselor, professor, and mentor, he made an enormous impact on the lives of others, an impact that continues to this day.[3]

GERALD BUSTIN: NATIONAL MENTOR

In 1995, 20,000 people gathered in a soccer field in Lae, Papua New Guinea, to hear an American executive speak about personal and spiritual growth. Forty-five buses were chartered to bring people to and from the venue. Local churches paid all expenses, including travel expenses for the guest speaker, Gerald Bustin.

Gerald Bustin

During his visit to Papua New Guinea, Gerald not only spoke to large crowds (often in their own languages), but also met with top government leaders regarding the ongoing work of the local churches in meeting the needs of their country. It was a reception few foreigners could expect to receive. As a result of his influence there, Gerald obtained a license to establish a Christian radio station that would be capable of reaching the population of the entire country—a major achievement in a nation that had never before had a full-time Christian radio station.

Mentoring in a Village

In 1958, a Chinese ship pulled up to the dock of Madang, a port of Papua New Guinea. Fourteen-year-old Gerald Bustin walked down the gangplank and onto the shore. The son of missionaries, he slept that night on the woven cane floor of a grass house, wrapped in a blanket to ward off the mountain cold. Soon after he began a remarkable work in this isolated country, meeting needs over the years as an entrepreneur, diplomat, urban leader, and executive.

Gerald initiated his work by living with the Kauapena people of the region of Papua New Guinea that is now known as the Southern Highlands. They were short, stocky, mountain people, living at elevations more than a mile above sea level. When Gerald arrived, the Kauapena used stone axes to cut their wood because they had not yet been introduced to steel. Neither had they discovered the wheel. Their weapons included their stone axes, knives made from bamboo, and arrows tipped with slivers of human bones. They worked their gardens with primitive bamboo tools.

Mentoring as an Entrepreneur

The work of Gerald and his colleagues centered on developing a business to meet the needs of the Kauapena. Gerald noticed that all the homes always had a cooking fire burning on the floor. The Kauapena typically threw away the ashes. Gerald saw an opportunity and offered to buy the ashes and then use them to fertilize some gardens. High in potassium and other minerals, the ash enriched the soil and increased the quality of the crops. Gerald then shipped the produce to the city by truck and reinvested the profits in the village, creating an economic cycle that benefited all involved. An unused resource was turned into profit and local workers received jobs. Gerald and his partners paid their costs and built the business, obtaining a fleet of large trucks in the process, some of which were purchased with cash.[4]

The villagers' earnings needed to be deposited in a safe place, so they started a branch bank in order to encourage people to save. Gerald was asked to manage the bank, something that served to develop his financial abilities. Managing a bank in a Kauapena village required more creativity than most bankers possess. Signatures, the standard sign of credibility, could not be used with people who could not write. Gerald and his partners created an alternative password system, encouraging individuals to use this method to gain access to their accounts.

Entrepreneurial businesses are necessary for future development in Papua New Guinea.

Mentoring as a Diplomat

This work in Papua New Guinea involved many personal challenges as well. The Kauapena people spoke the Imbogu language, a dialect that had never been written. The ordinary props of dictionary and grammatical diagrams were not available for this language. Day after day Gerald sat around the fires of the Kauapena people, repeating the words they said and writing down their language.

The time he invested in language learning was to pay large dividends in the future. On one occasion, the chief of the tribe Gerald was staying with discovered that a piece of his hair had been stolen. The villagers soon discovered who had committed this crime—the chief's hair was in the hands of a chief from an enemy tribe. Fear broke out in the village as the residents realized what had happened. They feared that the enemy's sorcerer would curse the hair, thus causing a curse to come to the chief and the entire tribe. The offended tribe sent an entourage to the enemy tribe, offering pigs in exchange for the piece of hair. This effort was not successful and tribal war broke out.

As he watched this senseless conflict, Gerald decided to try his hand at diplomacy. During the next few years, he became an ambassador, communicating between tribal governments to ease the tensions. He could speak their language, but the difference in his background gave him a neutral posture among warring groups. Much bloodshed was prevented as he exercised his intermediary skills in this way.

Mentoring as an Urban Leader

In 1969, Gerald moved near the city of Mendi to work with the Palime people. Once again he set up house in a local village, but this time he was not alone. It was his first home with his wife Roana, whom he had married on a visit to the United States. As a nurse, Roana became an integral part of the work, using her skills to care for the local people. The warmth of her personality would prove to be an asset in the years to come.

Papua New Guinea did not have enough high schools to meet student needs, and those that were in operation were in great demand. One of the high schools was

> Most mission efforts in the country were focused in the villages, reaching out to the rural poor. Gerald Bustin realized that by influencing leaders, he would eventually affect the wider rural populations as well.

located in the city of Mendi, not far from the village where Gerald lived. One Sunday, as Gerald opened services in the village church, he discovered that some visitors from the high school were present. They had walked over two hours in order to attend the service. The next Sunday they came again, showing genuine interest in the services. These were bright young men, destined to attend the university and later to receive top positions in the government.

A ministry idea began to form in Gerald's mind. He would start a church in the city, reaching business people and leaders in training. These groups were considered less important by those in traditional missions, so Gerald was introducing new demographics. Most mission efforts in the country were focused in the

> In particular, the church in Mt. Hagen became a place for young professionals to feel at home. In this way, the church helped to develop local leadership and to mentor a new generation of leaders to assume future positions of responsibility.

villages, reaching out to the rural poor. Gerald realized that by influencing leaders, he would eventually affect the wider rural populations as well.

The church Gerald started at Mendi became a spiritual home for the high school students who had come there to study. Especially popular among students were the food and fellowship to be found in the Bustin

Gerald and leaders in Papua New Guinea.

home. Gerald's pastoral care and Roana's winning ways made the students feel accepted in their home. Over several years the church grew and became a powerful force in the community. Teachers and students in the church moved on to top posts of leadership in the nation, carrying with them what they had learned in the church. A partial list of names includes Sir Wiwa Korowi, Governor General of Papua New Guinea (Queen Elizabeth's representative), Dr. Philip Kereme, Director of Higher Education in the country, Rev. Mondopa Mini, Director of the Papua New Guinea Bible Church (a denomination with 300+ indigenous members), and Wane Ninjipa, President of Pacific Bible College.

The church at Mendi launched the Bustins into a new sphere of influence. As the church grew and prospered, Gerald came to realize that he was most effective in the city. In 1979, he started a church in the city of Lae. At the same time, he began two other city churches: in Mt. Hagen (300 miles away) and in Port Moresby, the capital of Papua New Guinea. In both cases he sought local leaders to direct the ministries. Over time, the new churches grew and prospered, much as the Mendi church had done. Both churches planted other churches, reaching out to help many people in need. In particular, the church in Mt. Hagen became a place for young professionals to feel at home. In this way the church helped to develop local leadership and to mentor a new generation of leaders to assume future positions of responsibility.

Mentoring as an Executive

In 1983, Gerald moved back to the United States to become World Director of the Evangelical Bible Mission (now known as E.B.M. International). He left behind an amazing legacy. He had lived in Papua New Guinea for twenty-five years and had learned five of its languages. He had helped to start forty-two new churches and three businesses, including a bank, a grocery store, and a trucking company. In addition, he had started a boarding high school for local students who could not pass the government's high school exam. The Papua New Guinea Bible Church denomination had been placed under local leadership, giving Gerald and his foreign colleagues the opportunity to move on to other things. This denomination has since grown to become 600 churches strong.

As Director of Evangelical Bible Mission, Gerald sought to encourage others to make a difference as well. During the first eleven years he held this position, the number of missionaries the mission sent nearly quadrupled, growing from forty to one hundred forty missionaries active in the field.

Donations increased from $400,000 to almost $2 million per year. As a result of these increases, the mission has been able to initiate indigenous church movements in thirteen new fields, including the former Soviet Union, Fiji, and Brazil. Gerald has returned to Papua New Guinea on several occasions to speak and encourage people in the nation he knows so well.

Lessons in Mentoring from Gerald's Life

What can we learn from Gerald's life and work? He became part of the local system and learned the languages of those around him (some of them unwritten). This was tedious work, involving literally thousands of hours. He made the effort, committing to the local community and its needs. As part of the local system, he was able to play roles that were not indigenous to their societies, including those of entrepreneur, diplomat, and Christian witness.

Gerald realized that social change was inevitable, and positioned himself to take advantage of it. By moving his base to the cities, he helped develop leaders who would effectively administer the country. His investment paid off, and the values he shared have been spread to others, affecting their lives, work, and approach to governance. Gerald not only gave to the people in Papua New Guinea, but he also helped them to care for themselves. By promoting businesses and education, he developed their leadership skills, enabling them to combat poverty for themselves, their families, and the nation.

TABLE 7.3	
GERALD BUSTIN: LESSONS AND NEEDS	
Lessons to Learn	Become a part of the local system.
	Learn to work in different social environments.
	Develop local leaders.
	Study local culture.
	Learn the languages.
World Needs Addressed	Combated poverty.
	Created sustainable development.

DR. JUDITH D'AMICO: COMMUNITY ADVISOR

True Loyalties

In 2001, co-author John Johnson was in Haiti to teach a weeklong seminar on cross-cultural leadership. The classes met during the day, leaving the evenings free for social activities. One evening, he and one of his colleagues accepted an invitation to have dinner with an American physician who was working in the area. Arriving at her home, they discovered that she could not meet with them at the scheduled time, as a Haitian colleague had just come from another part of the country. He had traveled for hours over dangerous roads to seek her advice in a time of need. In a country with unreliable telephone service, she had no way of knowing he was coming.

Dr. Judith D'Amico

The American guests made their own arrangements for dinner that evening, but came away with a deep respect for a doctor who gave higher priority to Haitians in need than she did to her foreign guests. She had demonstrated in a powerful way her true loyalties. Those loyalties were with those she had been called to serve. She carried out this mission, even at the risk of offending her new friends.

This type of commitment and loyalty characterized Dr. Judith D'Amico's entire career. Born in Philadelphia, she attended school in Upper Darby, Pennsylvania. Her life was cross-cultural from the start, as her parents were Italian and her paternal grandfather could hardly speak English at all. As residents of a "WASP" neighborhood in Philadelphia, they were always treated like foreigners. The image of Italians as foreign outsiders stayed with her until she traveled to Italy during high school. As she visited the historical landmarks of her heritage, she realized that Italians were not outsiders. They were a people with a proud, rich heritage, one that had preceded her generation by literally thousands of years.

After graduating from Ursinus College, Judith attended medical school at the Hahneman College of Philadelphia. Shortly after graduation, she began her practice in Cleveland, Ohio. She discovered that she enjoyed the human interaction, but found traditional medicine repetitive and boring. She realized that she wanted to use her skills to improve health practices in her community, a function her traditional practice did not allow.

Advising in Africa

The year 1983 was to be a providential year in Judith's life. She traveled to Uganda twice on short-term mission trips with Africa Evangelical Enterprises. Upon arrival, she discovered a people who were suffering, both physically and emotionally. The brutal dictator Idi Amin had only recently gone into exile, leaving a legacy of murder and Stalin-style oppression in his wake. Judith and her team connected with local physicians to help provide a number of different immunizations. She discovered in the process that the public health system was well developed, but lacked resources to do the job. Judith and her colleagues provided thousands of immunizations and spiritual counsel as well.

As Judith worked among the needy in Africa, she began to sense a call to ministry, something she first had felt as a teenager. While in Uganda, she sensed a call to direct involvement, a directive to leave the comfort of an American doctor's life and instead offer her services to communities with greater needs, both in the United States and in other countries. This call changed her life.

Advising in Haiti

After much soul-searching and prayer, Judith moved to France in preparation for full-time work in Haiti. For eleven months she studied French and became familiar with Haitian culture. In spite of the rigorous study, she felt blessed to have the opportunity to prepare in this way. She would later learn that French not only would prepare her to communicate, but would serve as a professional credential in Haitian society as well. Formerly, Haiti had been a French colony. Members of the medical profession expected her to be able to communicate in the common business language they had been taught by their French colonizers many years before.

> "There is no way to adequately understand a culture and its people without being able to walk in the shoes of its language. It is through the eyes of language that one sees and experiences the worldview of the culture: its thinking, values, and raison d'etre."
>
> Dr. Judith D'Amico

A small basket-weaving business in Haiti.

Learning French was not difficult for Judith, but it was embarrassing. She came to language school with a good education, having graduated from two well-respected schools in the United States. Language learning forced her to take the role of a child again, making mistakes, learning new skills, and receiving frequent correction. It was a humbling experience (as it has been for the authors of this text), and even more so since the children of missionaries studying in the program bypassed the adults, achieving communication levels in weeks that took adults months to learn.

Haiti's other language is Creole, a mixture of French, Spanish, and English, with the grammatical structure of a West African tribal language. Judith also became fluent in this language, gaining much of her competence in the language from two mothers who worked in her home. Much of their conversation centered on the cultural norms for marriage, childbirth, and caring for children. The language and cultural information she learned in this way were crucial to her work among young mothers. She would later comment, "There is no way to adequately understand a culture and its people without being able to walk in the shoes of its language. It is through the eyes of language that one sees and experiences the worldview of the culture: its thinking, values, and raison d'etre."

Advising in Chicago

After three years of practicing medicine in Haiti, Judith accepted another assignment, this time in Chicago's inner city. She discovered that as Haitian mothers faced challenges, the residents of her Chicago neighborhood, West Garfield Park, did too. Once again she was the member of a minority group, one of a few white residents in a neighborhood of 30,000 African Americans. Her main focus was the health of two hundred teens who came to the clinic for prenatal care every year. The average age of her patients was twenty years, which meant that many of them were teenagers experiencing their first pregnancy. Most were young, scared, and without support from boyfriends (frequently local drug dealers) or families. At times the needs seemed endless.

In her work with young mothers, Judith was concerned with their spiritual as well as physical healing. In the examining room, she challenged them to be effective mothers and to make good decisions about their lives. Words gave way to drawings on paper as the empathetic physician took time to explain tough ideas. In describing this time, she notes, "Their faces would read, 'Dr. D'Amico, do you believe in me . . . that I can be a good mother, finish school, and go on to college?'" To this she would respond, "Of course I do!" She explains, "People were encouraged, women decided against abortion, spiritually oppressive illnesses were lifted, and some were physically healed during prayer."

> "Their faces would read, 'Dr. D'Amico, do you believe in me . . . that I can be a good mother, finish school, and go on to college?' "
>
> Dr. Judith D'Amico

Toward the end of her service there, urban researchers conducted a study comparing the results of her clinic with the local hospital's obstetrics unit. The results demonstrated that patients of the clinic, although drawn from the same neighborhood, had a five times better pregnancy outcome than did those of the hospital. Judith believes that it was not the medical care that made the difference, but the investment that was made, "an investment in West Garfield Park, one life at a time."

Advising in Alaska

In addition to locations where she was appreciated, Judith also experienced her share of challenging assignments. Her most difficult was in Bethel, Alaska. The darkness she experienced there was literal—in the winter months the sun did not shine for eighteen hours a day—but there was spiritual darkness as well.

During the winter in Bethel, Alaska, the sun does not shine for eighteen hours a day.

In her work she discovered that many of the spiritual problems manifested themselves in the tendency toward isolation. As she noted later, "I quickly learned that although the city had a population of several thousand people, the tendency was for people not to communicate with each other, even within the fifty-bed hospital."

Among the major reasons for this were years of conflict among the health care providers in the community, which included the state health care system, the hospital, and the community health workers.[5] Her initial ministry among them was to become "a human memo," going from one department to another with information, then asking managers to add to and build on what she brought to them. As an outsider to the conflict, she was eventually able to persuade some of the major players in the health care arena to meet face-to-face and attempt to resolve their differences. In this effort, she brought together the three factions. From the initial stages of the meetings, it was obvious that all three groups were adversaries, with years of misunderstanding among them.

Since they were afraid to vent their frustrations on one another (and then attempt to continue working together in the same health care district), they began to vent their frustrations on Judith. As an outside, temporary staff member, she became the scapegoat upon which the various factions could focus their frustrations. She describes these now as some of the most difficult meetings in which she has ever had to participate, either before or since. In spite of the pain, she sensed a special help, noting that the meetings "took a level of mediation far beyond what I would normally have possessed, especially since I had to chair and receive the brunt of their years of unresolved issues at the same time."

Several years after her short-term assignment in Alaska, she discovered that the three factions had learned to cooperate. The community workers, hospital, and the health care system came together to provide maternity care, which had been one of Judith's goals for them all along. Her prayers for the community were answered.

Advising Community Leaders

Seven years and seven days after leaving Haiti, Judith returned to live there again. After a term as director of the Albert Schweitzer Hospital in rural Haiti, she moved to the capital Port au Prince in the fall of 1999. She now serves as program director of Plan International Haiti, a non-governmental organization focusing on community health. Among other activities, this work manages 300 community health projects a year and a budget of $5 million. Plan International Haiti facilitates the fulfillment of her mission, which is to mentor, grow, and strengthen Haitian leaders.

Advice for Advisors

What can we learn from Judith's life? With a life of comfort at her disposal, she gave it up to address world need in Haiti, Alaska, and inner-city Chicago. In all of these contexts, she became not only a physician but a trusted community leader as well, bringing about positive change in cultures, organizations, and individuals. She became a part of the local system, learned the languages, and came to understand the cultures in which she served. In this way, she developed an awareness of individual cultural needs and amplified her opportunity to serve.

> Dr. Judith D'Amico accomplished change by pointing out to those with whom she worked the difference between where they were and where they could be.

Judith accomplished change by pointing out to those with whom she worked the difference between where they were and where they could be. Expertise power helped her bring about organizational change, as did her ability to network and develop helping relationships with others. Currently she is creating sustainable development by training local health professionals to meet the needs of others.

TABLE 7.4	
JUDITH D'AMICO: LESSONS AND NEEDS	
Lessons to Learn	Study culture and assess world needs for yourself.
	Be a friend, neighbor, mentor, and part of the community you want to help.
	Teach people to solve their own problems.
World Needs Addressed	Met health needs.
	Created sustainable development.

FACILITATING CHANGE IN OTHER CULTURES

The influence of the individuals we have profiled in this chapter reaches around the world. With a clear sense of world need, they have all addressed the problems their skills could help to solve. They took on new and different roles in the process, in some cases accomplishing what they were not originally trained to do. Using their skills, they have made a difference in the lives of thousands around the world. Yet, they are ordinary people. What they have done, we can do as well.

How can we make a difference? Chapter 8 explores this question, pointing out some specific ways to create change.

QUESTIONS FOR DISCUSSION

1. How did the individuals profiled in this chapter bring about change? Which of the approaches to change from chapters 4 and 5 do you see illustrated in their stories?

2. To which of these individuals do you most relate? What can you learn from their lives?

3. What fears do you have (if any) of living outside the United States? What anxieties might you need to overcome in order to move to another country?

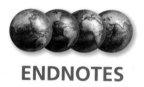

ENDNOTES

1. Listening in a local language would have made him suspect to the Lebanese.
2. Bob and others organized the CCX in Ukraine (*Spivdruzhnist Studentiv Khrystyan* or Union of Christian Students). This is a sister movement of the IFES (International Fellowship of Evangelical Students). More information about both groups can be found at http://www.ifesworld.org/defaulthome.asp.
3. If you would like to learn more about Bob's life, refer to his recent book, *I Am With You Wherever You Go* (Cupertino, CA: D.I.M.E. Publications, 2002). An earlier book is also available, *God and a Woman at Stanford: Reflections on the First One Hundred Years* (Cupertino, CA: D.I.M.E. Publications, 1991.) Contact D.I.M.E. Publishers at: P.O. Box 490, Cupertino, CA 95015, or email at books@dime.org.
4. Gerald asked us to make it clear to our readers that he did not work alone in developing this business and that he does not wish to take all the credit for what he was able to accomplish with the help of others.
5. This was a group of caregivers responsible for 100 villages scattered over 92,000 square miles of frozen tundra.

CHAPTER EIGHT

Application and Conclusion

ISSUES OF BREAD AND SALT

Before his pioneering efforts in India, Mahatma Gandhi first confronted discrimination in South Africa.[1] After finishing his work there, he returned home to India, where he was encouraged to become involved in politics. Instead, he went on a long journey through his homeland. His travels led him through the countryside, where he visited many villages and farms. He endured many unpleasant conditions as he patiently listened to the peasants and observed their surroundings.

Not long afterward, he attended a political convention. The country's top politicians gave rousing speeches for home rule and expulsion of the British. The audience was largely in agreement and loudly expressed support. Finally, the unpretentious Gandhi was given a chance to speak. When he was introduced, it was obvious that people were not interested. They left their seats and wandered around the convention floor.

Gandhi began his speech by talking about the real India. The real issue in India, he argued, was not about home rule. The citizens of India did not really care who ruled the country. What they did care about was bread and salt. Unless the politicians understood the issues of bread and salt—which clearly they did not—the voters would simply be replacing British tyrants with Indian tyrants. As Gandhi continued to speak, people returned to their seats and began to listen. Why? Because they were hearing something unusual, something of great importance—he was telling them the truth about their country. This unassuming man had found ways to understand their culture. He was now vocalizing it in a way they could feel and understand.[2]

Hundreds of millions of people in India still live in poverty.

Mahatma Gandhi succeeded because he understood that change efforts are more effective when based on accurate information. He understood that influencing others not only involves understanding change, but having the skills to learn about a culture as well. Observing the poor people of India set the foundation for his work, revealing their *actual* context, not what the politicians perceived it to be.

If we want to be effective change agents, we too need to know how to learn about a culture. In this way, we will make better decisions and achieve better results. This chapter will explore some of the many methods we can use to gather accurate information. We begin with more traditional methods of research, then discuss additional techniques, including observation, interviews, and ways to study organizations.

TOOLS FOR UNDERSTANDING CULTURE AND ORGANIZATIONS

How can we understand a culture that is not our own? This is not an easy task, but it can be done through careful preparation and research. In this section we will cover some approaches that have worked for others and provide practical advice regarding their implementation.

Ask the Right Question

Melvin and Carol Ember note, "Research projects work best if the researcher can state a clear, one-sentence question before starting. A good research question must be somewhere in the middle . . . not too large a question and not too small."[3] Examples of very broad questions include inquiries such as these: What is the meaning of life? Why does culture change? How do females differ from males?"

The problem with questions that are too broad in their scope is that we likely won't be able to find adequate answers for them. Doing a credible study of a large group of people requires an immense amount of time. Beginning researchers are better off to choose small groups to observe and to limit their observations to a few social settings. (See Table 8.1.) In this way, more accurate data can be obtained in a shorter period of time. Attempts can be made at a later date (or by another researcher) to generalize the information about the small group in order to apply it to other groups in the society.

TABLE 8.1	
SCOPE OF RESEARCH	**SOCIAL UNITS STUDIED**
Macro-Ethnography ↑ ↓ Micro-Ethnography	Complex society
	Multiple communities
	A single community study
	Multiple social institutions
	A single social institution
	Multiple social situations
	A single social situation

Source: James P. Spradley, *Participant Observation* (Orlando: Harcourt, Brace, Jovanovich, 1980), 30.

Starting with clearly focused questions, we can then begin the research task. Gathering basic information about a group of people can lead to an understanding of their needs, which in turn can suggest change methods (covered in chapters 4 and 5). It is a more objective way of beginning the change process, based on reliable data.

Choose a Research Focus

There are a great number of ways to learn about cultures other than our own, perhaps more than ever before. Articles and books abound, as well as a great deal of material on the Internet. It is important to note that if a significant amount of research has been done on a particular cultural group, it is far more time efficient to read existing studies than to collect primary data ourselves (by doing observations or interviews). (See Chart 8.1.)

Basic sources of cultural information include a number of yearbooks, world encyclopedias, and the Human Resource Area Files (HRAF), a rich collection of ethnographic writings from around the world. There are over one million pages in this collection, including ethnographies about little known people groups. Helpful books also include area studies, tourist guides, histories, and novels, all of which provide cultural insight. In many cases, specific books have been written about the culture of a country and how it differs from other countries. Other resources include books from the Intercultural Press of Yarmouth, Maine, the CultureGram series, and the Statesman's Yearbook. The number of relevant sites on the Internet is increasing every month, and a search by a country or region's name will provide vast quantities of important resources.

Study a Group's History

Studying the history of a culture is also a great asset in understanding the values of a country or people. For example, exploring the history of the United States (covered in chapter 2) helps one comprehend the pioneer spirit of this nation, the risk-taking involved, and the individualistic approach to life that characterizes many North Americans today. By examining a country's history and background, the characteristics of its people today make more sense, allowing for better decisions based on this information. We also can see how a society has changed over time, which provides additional insights.

We noted earlier that one of the greatest human resource problems faced by foreign companies in China has been hiring individuals who are willing to make

CHART 8.1 CHOOSING A RESEARCH FOCUS

Step 1: Answer the following question:

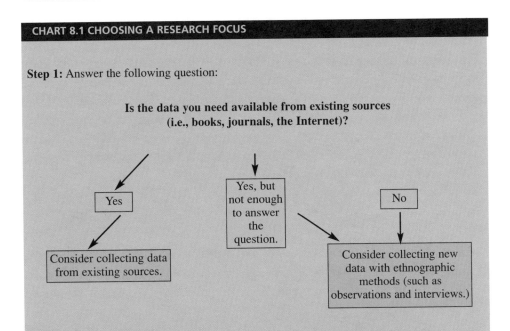

Is the data you need available from existing sources (i.e., books, journals, the Internet)?

Yes

Yes, but not enough to answer the question.

No

Consider collecting data from existing sources.

Consider collecting new data with ethnographic methods (such as observations and interviews.)

Step 2: Choose between a single social situation (i.e., one office, cafe, village square) and multiple social situations.

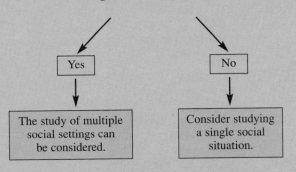

Do you have the time and resources available to collect data on a large number of participants?

Yes

No

The study of multiple social settings can be considered.

Consider studying a single social situation.

Note: No in-depth research project should be undertaken without training from professional researchers and consultation with some of the volumes that focus exclusively in this area, such as *Participant Observation* by James Spradley, *Cross-Cultural Research Methods* by Ember and Ember, or one of the other works written for the purpose of training students to do research.

independent decisions and to be creative in their approach. Understanding the history of China helps us understand the complexity of this challenge. Centuries of oppression culminated in the leadership of Communist Chairman Mao. Under his leadership, individuals were punished for decisive and/or creative action, the kind needed for private business to succeed. For generations before Mao, the Chinese developed the skills they needed to survive, most involving submission to the rule of an authoritarian ruler. Thus, history provides a clue as to why certain expectations exist in a culture, and this provides insights on what change approach will work best.

Learn the Value of Language

One of the most important aspects of being a cross-cultural change agent is to understand the language of those with whom we are working. This may seem

One of the most important aspects of being a cross-cultural change agent is to understand the language of those with whom we are working.

like a self-evident statement, but in a surprising number of cases, learning a local language is not seen as important. While Americans in other countries can generally get by without learning a local language, this can lead to misunderstanding and confusion.

Language learning helps us to understand the historical trends of the culture in which we are working. The history of a culture is often reflected in its language. For example, the term *"Slava Bogoo"* is a common expression in the Russian language. Its literal meaning is "Praise God" and it is used in place of exclamations in English, such as "That's great!" or "What good news!" or "I'm pleased to hear that." Its use has never been confined to a religious context, but is a common phrase in the speech of many different groups throughout Russian society, including atheists. A student of culture who understands language would trace the term back to an early period of Russian history, when the church was a force to be reckoned with in Slavic countries. The religious nature of the Russian people is still evident, despite seventy years of communism. The language itself points to seeds of Christian faith that did not die.

In many contexts, relating to individuals in their own language may not mean literally learning a new language. Almost every subculture and organization uses terms that are not understood by outsiders to the group. One of the best examples of this involves contemporary computer "geeks," whose ability to use unintelligible language is infamous. Those researching an organization learn the terms they need to know and use in order to be more of an insider. Relating may involve accents as well, either acquiring a regional accent or learning that the use of one is not associated with any particular personal characteristics.

Learn Through Observation and Interviews

Another important way to learn about cultures and organizations is by observing and asking key questions. Social scientists have traditionally called this method **ethnography**. Through careful observation, observers participate in a community to learn how it functions. This is important because although knowing the language can teach you many things about culture, even individuals fluent in language can make significant cultural mistakes. The lessons of history are invaluable but may not explain present-day behaviors. These limitations point to

> **ETHNOGRAPHY**
> The systematic study of other cultures, resulting in careful documentation.

the importance of cultural learning by observation, which provides cultural insights that cannot be gained any other way.

Observational learning can produce attitudinal change as well. In one of our classes, students from Eastern Europe were required to observe and interview Romans (commonly known as Gypsies) who sat on the floor of the local train station. This group was feared throughout the region and the students initially refused to have any contact with them. However, the students could not receive a passing grade without completing this assignment. After initial resistance, the learning they experienced from this assignment was phenomenal. Rather than encountering a dirty, dishonest people (as they assumed), they met a group of rather astute business travelers who were of Roman origin. An informative conversation with them ensued, and in the course of this discussion the students learned that many of the stereotypes about this group were wrong. The students' attitudes were changed through observational learning.

PRACTICAL ISSUES IN RESEARCHING

Choose the Subject(s) of Observation

The first two questions to answer regarding participant observation are:

1. Whom should I observe?

2. Where should I observe them?

In any culture, there are a bewildering number of answers to these questions. The answers depend on what we want to know and how much time we can invest in the project. It is important to choose a research issue that is of interest to us. What are the needs we are concerned about? What will help us assist others in their goals within the society? What will help us in our work? Research problems can be grand or simple, depending on the needs of the researcher involved. In many cases, researchers begin by defining one problem and then narrow it as they gain more information.

> It is important to choose a research issue that is of interest to us.

One of the key questions in observation is the question of access. Many social settings that might yield great results in learning are quite difficult to access. Co-author John Johnson once spent eight hours in order to gain a forty-five-minute interview with a high-level leader. While the interview was very productive, John abandoned the idea of studying this leader's organization because access was too difficult. The amount of time needed to gain access to those involved in the organization would have been greater than the information gained.

Another issue involves whether or not permission will be given to study a given social setting. Some settings require no permission (e.g., a public bus stop). Others require an easily obtained approval (schools, shops, hospital waiting rooms), while still others have restricted access. Restricted access situations generally require a

In some countries, researchers can only work with subjects of their own gender.

researcher to spend time and/or energy gaining the approvals that are needed to study a particular setting. In one of our classes, researchers who wished to study a bank found they were not allowed to observe or conduct interviews there. In another example, it took co-author Boyd Johnson over four months and a special trip to Africa to obtain a permit to carry out research in Tanzania. Other restricted access situations may include government offices, police operations, and any other social settings that afford exposure to classified company information.

Keep a Record of What You Observe

One of the most important aspects of participant observation is making a record of what is observed. In some settings, individuals feel comfortable speaking in front of a video camera or tape recorder, but in many others they do not. When those being observed do feel comfortable with such technology, its presence can significantly alter the nature of the interaction.

Aside from the use of recording equipment, there is no way to capture in words all of the events or interactions involved in a social setting, especially when researchers are actively involved themselves. In situations where notes are allowed, a condensed version of the main events can be recorded and expanded later into a more complete description. This becomes the main record of the event, one the observer references when producing the conclusions of the study.

In some situations, any type of data collection will alter the behaviors of participants in the situation. In such cases, the researcher should find a way to leave for a few moments and/or record the information as soon as possible after the event. Creating a good data record in such situations can be challenging indeed. Respect for the rights of those involved always prohibits the use of hidden cameras, recorders, or other devices.

Care must be taken both in gathering and recording accurate data.

Make a Record and Use What You Learn

What do we learn about a culture from our observations? Part of our learning will occur as we analyze the records we have made. As soon as possible after the observation session, it is important to rewrite field notes, describing every detail of the event as thoroughly as possible. It is important to do this while the event is still fresh. Experienced researchers allow time between interviews to commit what they have learned into text or record it verbally. Entering the write-up in a device that can be searched (for key words, etc.) makes the data much easier to find and summarize. Extensive research projects can involve thousands of observation notes, material that sometimes is difficult to classify and retrieve.

Records can be analyzed for key words, or for evidence that supports a thesis statement. The results can be summarized, reported to colleagues, or used as the basis of further observations. They help provide insight to individuals who need to know about a culture, but lack the time required for careful observation.

Research Methods for Studying Organizations

The research methods described above can be used to study either a culture or an organization. Regarding organizations, a number of other techniques are also helpful. One of the quickest and most helpful approaches for studying organizations is to make a decisions chart. (See Table 8.2.) On one side of the chart is a list of decisions to make; on the other side are the names of those who make these decisions. This chart can become an interview tool, helping the researcher discuss with the organization's members what kinds of power are being used within the organization. What types of power do those who make the decisions utilize? By interviewing participants about

TABLE 8.2	
DECISIONS TO BE MADE AND WHO MAKES THEM AT THE UNIVERSITY OF LENIN	
Decision to be Made	**Individual or Group Who Makes the Decision**
Hiring of the Rector	Minister of Education of the Country
Hiring of a Vice Rector	The Rector
Hiring of a new faculty member	Head of department in consultation with the Rector
Type of curriculum to use	Faculty Council
Who to admit into the university	Admissions Committee or the Rector and High Officials of the University
Permission to use one of the university's two copy machines	The Rector
Permission for a graduate student to have the use of a dormitory room	The Rector
Permission for a student to leave the program for a year	The Rector
Conferral of candidate of science degrees (similar to a doctorate in the U.S. system)	Governmental Education Committee
Decision to recommend that candidate of science degrees be conferred	Scientific Board composed of professors from the University of Lenin, but including professors from other universities as well
Selection of a chairperson for the Scientific Board	The Scientific Board
Number of hours a faculty person is required to teach	Head of his or her department

how decisions are made, we can often ascertain the perspectives of those who make the decisions.

Another helpful approach is to interview the members of the organization regarding what is involved in joining the organization and whether or not its members feel free to leave. Egalitarian and fatalistic organizations generally have extensive rituals for entering and leaving the organization, as well as a number of related organizational procedures. Those who leave before they are expected to do so may experience social stigma or shame. In individualistic organizations, members often perform one another's jobs. Roles are loosely defined and hierarchy almost nonexistent. Individuals can come and go as they please. The initiation rituals are informal or nonexistent and some individuals can leave without being noticed.

> It is important to realize that anyone engaged in participant observation potentially can face ethical questions.

A glance at the organizational chart may be helpful in determining whether or not an organization is hierarchical. Are there many levels in the organization? Do individuals in the organization spend time after hours in one another's company? In hierarchical organizations, this is rare. At work, each person occupies a specific role and understands the parameters of that role/level. There is little socializing after work. In many cases, individuals rarely see each other in a non-work setting. All of this is very helpful in assessing organizational cultures.

It is important to realize that anyone engaged in participant observation potentially can face ethical questions. When involved in ethnography or other kinds of research, it is important to let individuals know they are being studied and to collect data with their full recognition. Secret data-collecting devices may be effective for law enforcement, but will never be used by an ethical researcher. Individuals who may have made themselves vulnerable in the research must be protected and their privacy preserved, especially those who might lose their employment if researchers are careless or unethical in their research efforts.

Understanding Culture, a Bridge to Change

Understanding culture takes time, effort, and skill. Few people who develop an understanding of another culture do so without intentional effort in this area. By studying culture, we begin to understand a society's needs, which then allows us to expend our efforts in areas that truly matter.

Literature, language learning, and observation are important ways to bring

Learning about another culture may involve living with the people.

this about. Published literature can provide historical perspective and help us benefit from the experience of others. Observational learning teaches us sensitivity to behaviors and how to come to grips with the messages that come our way. Language learning embellishes this knowledge, enabling us to ask questions and explore. These areas give us different perspectives. Understanding all these areas in a more thorough way helps us realize that studying culture is an important tool in helping to produce change.

APPLYING THE LESSONS OF THIS BOOK

We set out at the beginning of this book to become better informed about the world. We learn in chapter 1 why this is important. The world is more interconnected than ever before; cultures, governments, economies, and religions of the world are all linked in new ways to each other. Chapter 2 demonstrates that we are all only pieces of the global picture. Whether we like it or not, we see the world through the prism of our own culture. Like individuals

The needs of the world should encourage us to assist in making positive change.

from other nations, the people of the United States have a history that has shaped them, a pride regarding their culture, and a set of values uniquely their own.

But understanding ourselves is not enough. We learn in chapter 3 that the needs of the world demand a response. As we come to understand the problems that confront the world, we realize that they are *our* problems as well. Because of travel and trade, international borders of the world are more porous than ever before. And the trends toward globalization described in chapter 1 mean that there is no way to insulate ourselves from the hunger, poverty, and spiritual need of other nations. As clearly shown by the Asian financial crisis of 1997, for example, economic problems in other countries inevitably will affect us too.

In chapters 4 and 5, we learn more about change. How do cultures change, and how are change initiatives enacted in organizations? We explore various answers to these questions as we survey different ways in which change has been accomplished. We (examine) strategies for bringing it about in cultures and individuals. In chapters 6 and 7, we meet seven individuals who have made an impact on the world through their gifted lives. They studied the culture around them, developed the skills they needed, and made a difference in the lives of others. They are ordinary people, yet through their sincere efforts they accomplished change in nations, cities, villages, and families. What they have done, we can do as well.

Using This Book to Facilitate Change in the United States

How can we make a difference in the world? For most people, this begins at home. If we live in the United States, the growing diversity gives us daily opportunities to come in contact with individuals from other cultures, whether at work, in school, or in family or community events. These connections should be nourished. Given the right encouragement, they can become channels of friendship, learning, and mutual understanding. Many of those who come here from other countries are lonely and want more interaction with local people. If we choose to do so, we can be positively influenced by them and have an equally beneficial impact on their lives.

Business people from other countries often struggle for acceptance in the United States. Most of them who live in America would appreciate more contact with individuals from their communities. One result of globalization is the fact that even smaller American cities may have a Chinese restaurant, an Hispanic church, or a medical clinic operated by physicians from India. Rather than avoid contact with "foreign" people, seek ways to be involved in their lives. Using the techniques presented earlier in this chapter, we can study their cultures and organizations, and perhaps learn about international issues in the process.

Another way to influence our communities is to take advantage of local

Total immersion language learning is available in many countries, including Guatemala.

opportunities to learn a language. One example is a businessperson in a small city in Indiana, who became acquainted with people from a small community of migrant workers. He taught himself Spanish and began to talk to them. Eventually he was able to engage in regular conversation with members of the Hispanic community in his city (and became fluent in the language). Through this dialogue, he was able to help them bring about positive change in their lives.

Individuals who wish to learn a language quickly should take advantage of the total immersion language programs that operate in Mexico, Guatemala, Honduras, and French-speaking Canada.[4] Such language schools not only provide instruction, but also make arrangements for housing with non-English-speaking families. The lower cost of living in many countries makes language learning affordable—in many cases, it is cheaper to be a language student in another country than it is to live in the United States. Most language learners progress rapidly in total immersion environments. By studying at such a school in Guatemala, co-author John Johnson became conversational in Spanish in three months, having never studied it before in the United States. Co-author Boyd Johnson engaged in language immersion study in Thailand and found it was the only way for him to learn Thai.

Using This Book to Facilitate Change in Other Countries

The three individuals profiled in chapter 7 made an impact on their world through long-term international assignments. Over a period of years, they honed their professional skills, increasing their ability to serve others in a significant way. As a result of this preparation, they have had the opportunity to accept assignments in other countries. Not everyone can serve in this way, but those who do accept the challenge have the opportunity to make a significant impact in the world. Individuals who wish to practice their professional skills in another country (and be paid for doing so) should consider preparing to work in medicine, higher education, international economics, business, and development.[5] A huge nonprofit sector exists as well, doing work in virtually all nations. Some of these are paid positions, and some require workers to raise their own support. Most of the latter organizations provide training in how to raise funds for these kinds of assignments.

One effect of globalization is the fact that it is no longer difficult to find employment outside the United States. While not everyone can obtain a job overseas, finding a job in another country is actually not that difficult. For example, you can easily obtain an English teaching job for six months to a year through the Internet. In many cases, a basic high school education is all that is

Getting to know people from other cultures is a very rewarding experience.

required. International schools in other countries are in constant need of teachers (with education degrees) who can teach the children of diplomats, business people, and missionaries. Agricultural jobs are sometimes available in other countries as well.[6] The lower salaries paid for such assignments are often compensated by a lower cost of living, especially in developing countries.

Short-term volunteer assignments in other countries have become very common and are greatly available in today's world. A high percentage of college students currently spend a few weeks learning outside the United States during the course of their degree programs. Groups of professionals often travel to other countries to donate their services for a few weeks to those with needs (such as those who have gone on trips with Ray and Barb Schulz). And a plethora of short-term missionaries flood the airways every summer, doing everything from building houses to helping in schools.

In most cases, serving for a few weeks is better than not being able to serve at all. Professionals often can provide services that are wanted and needed in the host country. But all short-term visitors to another country must be sure to assess before they go whether or not they have skills that are needed by locals. Short-term volunteers who fail to explore this question may take jobs away from people in the local economy who really need them.

Opportunities to stay current regarding the needs of the world come to us through print and media sources. One positive result of the September 11 tragedy in New York is the increased attention to international news in our newspapers and television programs. National Public Radio, available in most communities, has long been a source of international news for those who want to stay informed in this area.[7] The History Channel often features programs with an emphasis on international history. It is possible to have one-on-one conversations with people all over the world through E-mail, bulletin board, and chat rooms. It is not uncommon for those researching a particular country to e-mail someone in that country and obtain information directly. Chambers of Commerce in different nations are happy to connect foreign businesspeople to their local communities. Most U.S. embassies abroad have a commerce section that specializes in creating interaction between the businesspeople of the country and interested individuals in the United States.

What Can *You* Do?

At the beginning of this book, we discussed the contrast between the rich and the poor in Bangkok, witnessed by Boyd Johnson. As a theme throughout

Every person can make some contribution to improve the world.

the chapters, we have seen that these extremes exist everywhere; this example is just a microcosm of the true condition of people around the world. Many problems exist and the idea of making a difference may seem difficult, if not impossible. But, in reality, all efforts *are* important. Every person can make some contribution to improving the world, and the combined efforts of many people can truly bring about global change.

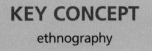

KEY CONCEPT
ethnography

Now what will you do to change the world? Globalization and technology provide many opportunities to influence the lives of others. How will you take advantage of them? We all have different skills, backgrounds, and interests. Therefore, we will not all serve in the same way. But there *is* a place for you, an opportunity waiting for your talents, enabling you to serve the world.

QUESTIONS FOR DISCUSSION

1. What cultural research topic interests you? How could you create a study for this topic?

2. What methods are available to you if you were to learn a foreign language? Which language would be most useful for you to learn?

3. Would you be willing to live or work in another culture? What unique gifts and talents do you have that could contribute to global change?

ENDNOTES

1. As we saw in the previous chapter, he chose to be buried in Africa as a sign of his concern for those beyond the perimeters of his homeland.
2. As told in Robert E. Quinn, *Deep Change: Discovering the Leader Within* (San Francisco: Jossey-Bass, 1996), 199-200.
3. Carol R. Ember and Melvin Ember, *Cross-Cultural Research Methods* (Walnut Creek, CA: Alta Mira Press, 2001), 21.
4. An Internet search with the keywords "Learning Spanish" or "Learning French" will produce web sites and E-mail addresses of language schools in countries bordering the United States.
5. Corporate assignments in other countries are generally well paid and often provide professionals with a higher standard of living than they would have in the United States.
6. Good sources for obtaining information about international jobs are the Lonely Planet sites on the Internet.
7. The call numbers for your local station can be obtained on the Internet at npr.org.

Glossary

achievement
Result gained by effort.

adversaries
Decision makers with whom we do not experience agreement or trust.

allies
Decision makers with whom we experience agreement and trust.

apartheid
Legally sanctioned racial segregation.

autonomous society
Individuals or groups who live separated from the larger society and who have little or no interaction with others.

bedfellows
Decisions makers with whom we generally experience agreement but little trust.

caste system
A system of social class and status that is determined by birth and fixed for life.

Christian social activism
The belief that Christians are given the duty to help those whose problems are caused by social injustice and Western exploitation.

coercive power
The ability to force someone in an organization to do something, even against that person's will.

culture
A particular society or group's way of life, including the values, beliefs, and norms of behavior it passes on to future generations.

demographic collapse
When the reproductive rate is so low that the population declines.

egalitarian society
A group-oriented society marked by similar status levels; often considered closed to outsiders.

entrepreneurial
Enterprising; a trait of one who makes the most of an opportunity, even if it involves risk; the ability to create an enterprise.

ethnic culture
The identities and practices that people derive from an ethnic group.

ethnocentrism
The belief that one's own group is the standard by which all others should be judged.

ethnography
The systematic study of other cultures, resulting in careful documentation.

evolutionary change model
A change model predicated on unilinear development; that is, societies develop in a series of stages, usually from primitive to advanced.

expert power

The power invested in someone who has expertise that is scarce in the organization.

extended family

A family group that is larger than the nuclear family (mother, father, children) and that includes other close relatives.

fatalistic society

A highly structured society that is difficult to enter or leave.

fence-sitters

Decisions makers about whom we are uncertain regarding agreement and trust issues.

fieldwork

A method of investigation based upon firsthand observation and collection of information in the field.

functional change model

A change model based on the functions of each part of a society.

globalization

The increasing awareness and interaction of individuals, organizations, and businesses in an international context.

global warming

The rise in global temperatures attributed to the rise of atmospheric carbon dioxide levels.

hierarchical society

A structured society in which individuals function at different levels or in different categories with dissimilar status.

homogeneous

Of the same or similar kind. In a homogeneous population, the people are ethnically similar.

human resource perspective
Views organizations as meeting human needs; particularly capitalizes on the fit between the organization and its members.

ideology
Ideas, concepts, or goals that distinguish one group or culture from another; core beliefs.

indigenous
Originating in or occurring naturally in a particular region.

individualism
The belief that individual needs take priority over the group's needs, and that each person is responsible for him/herself, basing decisions on individual perceptions and needs.

individualistic change model
A change model based on the relationship of individual action to group custom and tradition.

individualistic society
A society based on freedom of choice and the autonomy of its individual members.

interactionist change model
A change model based on how a culture changes because of its interaction with the outside world.

LDCs
An acronym for less developed countries.

meritocracy
The advancement of people due to achievement, not social background or privilege.

MNCs
An acronym for multinational corporations.

nation
A group of people composed of one or more nationalities and possessing a defined territory and form of government.

opponents
Decision makers with whom we experience trust but not agreement.

parochialism
Limited in range or scope; a restricted view of the world; provincial, narrow-minded.

political perspective
Views organizations as political arenas in which individuals, coalitions, and interest groups compete for the organization's scarce resources.

position power
The power invested in one who holds a position of authority in an organization.

pragmatic worldview
An attitude that emphasizes practical solutions to problems.

reference power
The power invested in someone who can recommend or positively reference someone else.

religious totalitarianism
The situation that occurs when a particular religious group imposes its ideology on others, usually by force.

resistance power
The power of refusal vested in those who unite with others in the organization to achieve an objective.

reward power
The power invested in one who distributes compensation or other nonmonetary rewards to others in the organization.

self-reliance
Confidence in and dependence on one's own efforts and/or abilities.

structural perspective
Views organizations as structures designed to organize activity into levels and roles, clearly defining relationships of organizational members.

sustainable development
Community development that can be continued by local people, mainly with local resources.

symbolic change model
A change model based on a culture's reaction to new symbols and rules of behavior.

symbolic perspective
Views organizations as places to help people find meaning through symbols, ceremonies, and stories.

Two-Thirds World
Those countries in which the majority of the population lives in poverty. About two-thirds of the world's countries fall into this category.

upward mobility
The ability to rise to a higher social or economic position.

World Trade Organization (WTO)
An international body that determines rules for global trade. It is comprised of most of the world's industrial nations.

worldview
The way people see the world and their place in it.

Index

H

J

K

L

NOTES

NOTES

NOTES

NOTES

ABOUT THE AUTHORS

Boyd Johnson, Ph.D., is an associate professor of international studies at Indiana Wesleyan University, where he teaches global issues and social science courses. His doctorate is in international studies. He previously worked for World Vision, first as a researcher at the International Office and later as Associate Director of Leadership (South Pacific), Operations (Thailand), and Training (South Asia Region). He then became the Field Director in Pakistan and later served as Director of Strategic Resources for World Vision Canada. He worked in international development for sixteen years, a position that took him to over fifty countries on all continents. He lived for thirteen years in Australia, Thailand, Pakistan, Singapore, and Canada. He also designed many community development programs and has served as a consultant to global businesses and aid agencies.

John S. Johnson, Ph.D., is a member of the business faculty at Indiana Wesleyan University, where he currently teaches International Management and Organizational Behavior. He is also a human resource analyst for Global Talent International, an Indiana-based training and recruiting company. His doctorate is in intercultural education, with a focus on organizational leadership. He also holds a master's degree in human resource leadership. Previously, he worked for the International Institute for Cooperative Studies, training business people in the Ukraine for five years. As a professor at Azusa Pacific University, he conducted leadership seminars for business people and nonprofit leaders around the world. During the seven years that he resided outside the United States, he lived in Guatemala, Nigeria, England, and Ukraine, and visited over forty countries.